# WALK THE TODDS

£2 sale

Todd's first trig point on Cannock Chase near his home.

ISBN 978-1-5272-7234-7

**DISCLAIMER**

Every effort has been made to describe these walks as accurately and honestly as possible. All the walks have been described in reasonably good conditions and doing them during the Winter months could make them considerably more difficult. Weather can change quickly and dramatically at any time of year and affect walking conditions at any time. Sections of these walks can change over time, for example, Stiles, Gates, Fences and Forestry can all be altered over the years.

The choice to tackle these walks and use this book is your own responsibility as is your confidence in your own ability to navigate these walks and maintain your safety and the safety of others while out in the mountains.

With all these points in mind the Author, Publisher, any contributor to this book and Todd himself can accept no responsibility for any loss, damage, injury or death to yourself or others which may arise from choosing to use this book on your walks.

The North Wales Mountain Rescue Association (NWMRA) supports rescue teams that cover over 75% of the walks in this book. We have been visiting this area for almost 20 years and it is where Todd does most of his walking. Please read page 140 in this book and also visit the NWMRA website and donate to assist these teams.

*Front cover picture: Todd on Carnedd y Filiast looking to Elidir Fawr, Walk 15*
*Rear cover picture: Todd on Moelwyn Mawr, Walk 18*

Designed and produced by John Griffiths. Printed in the UK.

# CONTENTS

## KEY FOR MAPS

●      Highest 50 summits

●      Minor summits

**P**      Car park, start and finish of walk

– – ➤ – –   Route of walk

– – ➤ – –   Possible alternative return route

# ACKNOWLEDGEMENTS & DEDICATIONS

I would like to dedicate this book to my Grandchildren Lexi, Coni, Luca, Dolores, Walter, Bonnie and any more that may arrive after the book is published. I would also like to challenge them all to complete these walks when they are old enough, sadly I don't think Todd will be around to guide them but I have no doubt that each walk would improve their lives.

I would also like to dedicate this book to my wife Gail and say thank you for letting her dog Todd create these adventures. It would not have been possible to complete without her help and support for each walk and the overall construction of the book. She was thought about on every walk and we toasted her on every summit, me with a bottle of water and Todd with a Wainwright biscuit and the occasional leg cocking.

Thank you also to my good friends Jim and Linda Hooper, widely acknowledged as Cannock's leading Mountaineers. Without their advice and inspiration many years ago I probably would never have set foot on a Mountain at all. They have also been a great support throughout each walk, editing photos as we went, from the red room at Anfield.

I must also thank the other contributors to the book, Stephen Jones, a qualified Mountain leader of Anelu Aim Higher and his invaluable advice on Mountain safety and Hattie Bertenshaw, a qualified Vet and Mountain Rescue member for her advice on the suitability of dogs for these walks, also Chris Lloyd of NWMRA. The man responsible for expertly compiling this book is John Griffiths, a big thank you to John for all his advice and patience, not forgetting his wife Margaret and her hospitality while listening to us discussing mountains and football.

Last but certainly not least, Todd himself, he is the star of the show and there would definitely be no book without him. If you are a dog owner then you are well aware of what your dog does or doesn't like and I know for a fact that Todd has enjoyed every inch of these walks. He has also given me hours of pleasure watching his antics and hours of grief trying to keep him away from sheep, if you are a solo walker like me get yourself a Border Terrier and as Jim and Linda would say "You'll never walk alone".

*Owner Gail with Todd on Snowdon near the famous H.*

*Todd as a puppy, he was born on 1st November 2014 in Uttoxeter, Staffordshire. His posh name is* **Morpheus Marcasite,** *roughly translated it means "Stony God of sleep", usually after a walk!*
*Todd was named after our close family friend Todd Cooke, Border Terrier specialist and ex-breeder. He actually picked Todd out of the litter. A good choice if I say so myself!*

# WALKING THE TODDS

The title of this book *'Walking the Todd's'* is not an attempt to give this particular group of mountains a name. Once I had started this project and family members knew what the aim was, the following questions began to be asked:- When is your next Todd? How many Todd's have you done now? Are you doing a Todd this week? How is Todd coping on the Todd's? When will you finish the Todd's, and so on.

The book had started out as *'Todd's Travels'* but all the questions provoked the name change as the book took over our walking lives.

## SELECTION OF ROUTES

There are many routes to all of the summits in this book. The ones Todd and I have chosen are designed to give a good day out with a mainly circular route back to your starting point without the fuss of public transport or using two vehicles.

If you are just summit bagging then there are quicker options by either doing an out and back walk or selecting a different route altogether. Some of the walks could be joined together to make a longer day and gain more summits but if you do have your dog with you please consider whether that is suitable for them.

There is no easy way to complete any of these Walks. Your dog will need to be fit and suitable to the terrain and distance involved. If you have any doubts then don't take them with you, it's not worth it. The last thing I want to do is to encourage people to take their dog where they really shouldn't.

## TIMES, DISTANCES AND MAPS

The times given for each walk will vary depending on your own ability and ambition. Many people set themselves a target and equally as many people like to take their time and enjoy everything that is around them. Always allow a good half a day and in some cases a full day for these walks.

The distances are reasonably accurate but will again vary for a number of reasons, people taking shortcuts or exploring along the route and the fact that there is a choice of return routes for some of the walks.

There are many maps available for all of these walks, the ones listed are well known but you should select a map you are comfortable with and confident you can use it with your compass. There are also many guide books available and I have always found reading a couple of them leading up to a walk gives you good knowledge of your route before you set off.

The small maps in this book are not to scale and only a guide to use in conjunction with the pictures and information on each walk.

## TECHNOLOGY

In addition to maps there are plenty of navigational devices and apps available in todays technical world. A lot of these are wonderful aids to our days out off the beaten track, some people are shy of them and some people love them. They all require a power source so if you are using one please make sure you have spare battery capacity or charging unit. Always have your map and compass with you, no batteries required for these unless you need a torch to see them.

# HIGHEST 50 SUMMITS
## Throughout Wales in height order

There seems to be conflicting evidence of the actual order of the highest summits in Wales. The list I have used for this book has been compiled using several different versions used in other publications and on web sites. Some peaks have more than one summit, 'North top – South top etc' but for this book one summit only per peak is listed and the other summits visited will be referred to in the text with each walk.

### Crib Goch

I'm sure most of you are aware of the name Crib Goch, the famous ridge which is part of the Snowdon Horseshoe. Although it is number 14 on this list I have not used it in the walks as I believe there are places on the route far too dangerous to take a dog. In my opinion the dog could be a danger to itself, its owner and anyone else in the vicinity at that time. This is why I have included Drosgl at number 51 in the list to make up the 50 main summits visited on these walks. I could have done Crib Goch on my own with the camera and included it in the walks but that would have been cheating on Todd, after all it is his book.

Uncle Glen on Crib Goch, not a place for dogs, in my opinion.

| Peak | | Range | Height | | Walk |
| --- | --- | --- | --- | --- | --- |
| | | | Metres | Feet | No. |
| 1 | Snowdon | Snowdon | 1085 | 3561 | 20 |
| 2 | Garnedd Ugain | Snowdon | 1066 | 3499 | 20 |
| 3 | Carnedd Llywelyn | Carneddau | 1064 | 3492 | 10 |
| 4 | Carnedd Dafydd | Carneddau | 1040 | 3413 | 10 |
| 5 | Glyder Fawr | Glyderau | 999 | 3279 | 2 |
| 6 | Glyder Fach | Glyderau | 990 | 3249 | 2 |
| 7 | Pen yr Ole Wen | Carneddau | 978 | 3210 | 10 |
| 8 | Foel Grach | Carneddau | 976 | 3203 | 7 |
| 9 | Yr Elen | Carneddau | 962 | 3157 | 7 |
| 10 | Y Garn | Glyderau | 947 | 3108 | 14 |
| 11 | Foel Fras | Carneddau | 942 | 3091 | 12 |
| 12 | Carnedd Gwenllian | Carneddau | 926 | 3039 | 7 |
| 13 | Elidir Fawr | Glyderau | 924 | 3033 | 15 |
| 14 | Crib Goch | Snowdon | 923 | 3029 | ---- |
| 15 | Tryfan | Glyderau | 917 | 3003 | 24 |

| Peak | | Range | Height | | Walk |
| --- | --- | --- | --- | --- | --- |
| | | | Metres | Feet | No. |
| 16 | Aran Fawddwy | Aran | 905 | 2970 | 16 |
| 17 | Y LLiwedd | Snowdon | 898 | 2947 | 20 |
| 18 | Penygadair | Cadir Idris | 893 | 2913 | 8 |
| 19 | Pen y Fan | Brecon Beacons | 886 | 2907 | 5 |
| 20 | Aran Benllyn | Aran | 885 | 2905 | 3 |
| 21 | Corn Du | Brecon Beacons | 873 | 2864 | 5 |
| 22 | Moel Siabod | Moelwynion | 872 | 2861 | 1 |
| 23 | Erw Ddafad Ddu | Aran | 870 | 2855 | 3 |
| 24 | Mynydd Moel | Cadir Idris | 863 | 2832 | 8 |
| 25 | Arenig Fawr | Arenig | 854 | 2802 | 23 |
| 26 | Llwytmor | Carneddau | 849 | 2786 | 12 |
| 27 | Pen yr Helgi Du | Carneddau | 833 | 2734 | 11 |
| 28 | Foel Goch | Glyderau | 831 | 2727 | 14 |
| 29 | Cadair Berwyn | Berwyn | 830 | 2724 | 4 |
| 30 | Moel Sych | Berwyn | 827 | 2714 | 4 |
| 31 | Carnedd y Filiast | Glyderau | 822 | 2698 | 15 |
| 32 | Mynydd Perfedd | Glyderau | 822 | 2698 | 15 |
| 33 | Waun Fach | Black Mountains | 811 | 2662 | 13 |
| 34 | Cyfrwy | Cadir Idris | 811 | 2662 | 19 |
| 35 | Bera Bach | Carneddau | 807 | 2648 | 22 |
| 36 | Y Foel Goch | Glyderau | 805 | 2642 | 6 |
| 37 | Fan Brycheiniog | Carmarthen Fans | 802 | 2632 | 21 |
| 38 | Pen y Gadair Fawr | Black Mountains | 800 | 2626 | 13 |
| 39 | Pen Llithrig y Wrach | Carneddau | 799 | 2622 | 11 |
| 40 | Cribyn | Brecon Beacons | 795 | 2609 | 5 |
| 41 | Bera Mawr | Carneddau | 794 | 2606 | 22 |
| 42 | Mynydd Pencoed | Cadir Idris | 791 | 2596 | 8 |
| 43 | Moel Hebog | Eifionydd | 783 | 2569 | 17 |
| 44 | Glasgwm | Aran | 780 | 2560 | 16 |
| 45 | Cadar Bronwen | Berwyn | 780 | 2559 | 4 |
| 46 | Moelwyn Mawr | Moelwynion | 770 | 2527 | 18 |
| 47 | Waun Rydd | Brecon Beacons | 769 | 2524 | 9 |
| 48 | Gallt yr Ogof | Glyderau | 763 | 2504 | 6 |
| 49 | Fan Hir | Carmarthen Fans | 760 | 2494 | 21 |
| 50 | Drum | Carneddau | 760 | 2494 | 12 |
| 51 | Drosgl | Carneddau | 758 | 2488 | 7/22 |

# WALK PREPARATION

Please don't underestimate any of these walks. None of them are an easy stroll in the park and they all deserve planning and respect before you take them on. A lot of the walks are in remote areas and you can go a long time without seeing anyone else. Having said that though, all of the walks will reward you for your efforts with stunning scenery, spectacular views and a real sense of achievement. Pick a fine clear day and this book will guide you on your way, but as we all know conditions in the hills can change rapidly and in cloudy conditions the book will be no good on its own, it will not help you if you become lost especially in poor visibility. You need to make sure you have other navigational skills, especially how to use a Map and Compass, please read the section from Stephen Jones of Anelu Aim Higher on pages 14 to 16 and follow his advice. Too many people have had to call out Mountain Rescue Teams because they are lost. Along with your Map and Compass you should also have a Headtorch, Whistle and First Aid Kit, these items are no carriage and could prove invaluable.

Always take enough food, drink and additional, warm, waterproof clothing with you. Strong appropriate footwear is also essential as you will encounter all types of terrain, wet ground, scree and rocky sections where your hands will be needed for some mild scrambling. It's no good turning up in slippers, carrying a handbag. You should also bear in mind that during the Winter months these walks become a completely different challenge, think carefully before you go and research what you need before venturing up high at that time of the Year.

Please research each walk before you go, use the internet, text books and any other source of information you can find, it will all assist you on your journey. Don't underestimate the weather, check all the forecasts carefully, I have been misled on several occasions and if conditions do deteriorate don't ever be afraid or too proud to turn back, the walk will be there another day.

I have always thought the most difficult route finding on a walk is at the start, so many paths, roads and obstacles it's easy to take the wrong turn. Once a decent bit of height is gained the route tends to open up often giving views of your targets ahead and in some cases your route back down. This is why I have used so many pictures early in the walk where mistakes can easily be made, setting you off in the wrong direction.

Hopefully all the pictures will make your route finding easier and assure you that you are on the right place at various points throughout your journey.

Enjoy your walking.

## MOUNTAIN RESCUE

Hopefully, you will never need them but there are many different Rescue Teams covering all the walks in this book. There are too many numbers to list each one individually but if you need to contact them the following applies.

CALL 999 or 112 and ask for the POLICE and MOUNTAIN RESCUE then follow their instructions and be prepared to describe your journey and the situation you find yourself in. You can find out more about Mountain Rescue by following this link.

### https://www.mountain.rescue.org.uk/teams/

Please read page 140 and if possible donate to assist these rescue teams.

# PREPARATON FOR TODD

Todd is a fit Border Terrier in the prime of his life and coped with these walks easily, very often still striding out ahead at the end of the walk.

Please don't assume that all dogs are capable of completing these walks and maybe seek advice from your own vet if you are taking a dog with you. I have seen many dogs, led by unthoughtful owners into terrain that they are not suited to. Long legged dogs struggling over rocks, heavy dogs desperate for a drink and dogs with restricted breathing not coping with the distance they are being taken.

Please give some thought before you take your dog with you and read the article by Harriet Bertenshaw, Vet and Mountain Rescue Volunteer on page 12, the last thing I want to do is put anyone's dog into a situation it's not suitable for just because the owner likes the pictures in this book and wants to see their dog on one of the summit cairns.

I have always followed the same rules when thinking of taking Todd a long distance.

1. A strong body harness, as a collar can lead to a neck strain on steep ground.

2. A spare lead, Todd would definitely chase sheep.

3. A jacket, just in case the weather changes for the worst while you are out, preferably a warm, waterproof and high visibility one.

4. Food, it's a long day and a lot of energy is spent. I would never walk him on a full stomach but just drip feed him throughout the walk.

5. Plenty of water, don't rely on streams, pools etc and make time to stop for a drink.

6. I know we like clear weather for a walk but if it is too hot then don't take the dog. Generally if it's forecast over 20 degrees then I wouldn't take Todd any distance. Remember you are in the open for long periods, no shade to hide in and on rocky terrain the dogs paws will feel a hot surface.

Some of these points may sound trivial but I once saw a Bull Mastiff on high ground desperate for a drink, his owner had all his fancy walking clothes but no water, he tucked his shirt in while I gave his dog a drink, selfish or what!

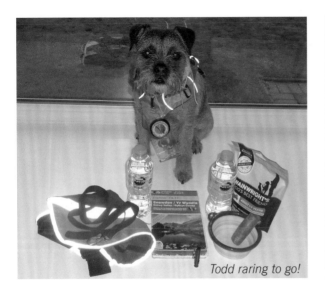

*Todd raring to go!*

**Please check with your own vet that your dog is capable of these walks before you take them on.**

# LIVESTOCK ADVICE

All of these walks will bring you into contact with Livestock and Wild Birds. There are many incidents each year of sheep being attacked by dogs and some farmers will shoot your dog if it is harassing their animals. Below are some signs that are found at various locations throughout these walks, please take notice of them, respect the farmers livelihood and the welfare of all the animals. It's easier just to keep your dog on a lead.

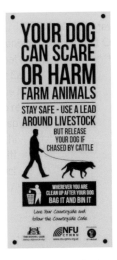

---

# SHEEP TICKS

After walking in all these areas please check your dog for sheep ticks. They can be picked up throughout the year but are most common between Spring and Autumn. They can infect your dog if not removed within a short space of time. There is plenty of information on the internet on how to locate and remove these ticks. Do not be tempted to pull them out or crush them as they need to be completely removed. A special tool is available for this, you can always contact your Vet for advice.

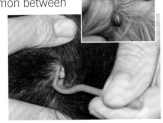

# CARE FOR YOUR DOG IN THE MOUNTAINS

As stated at the front of the book, the terrain and distance involved make these walks a tough proposition. However, as the author rightly points out, that with proper preparation, knowledge, equipment and the right dog then twenty four rewarding days out can be achieved.

As a qualified Vet, Mountain Rescue Volunteer and Dog Handler I would like to point out that all dogs are not suitable for these walks. Many times Mountain Rescue Teams have been called out to rescue someone's dog, not because of an accident, but because the animal is exhausted and unable to continue, that cannot be fair on the animal or the team called out to rescue it.

Many dogs will cope with these walks with no problem but equally many will not. The distances are long, the rocky terrain is difficult and there are many stiles, wet areas, walls and steep sections to negotiate. If you do decide to take your dog on these walks please consult with your own vet beforehand as to whether they are capable of what lies ahead.

Once you have established your dog is suitable please make sure food and water is available for them as you may be out for some considerable time. Never take your dog walking on a full stomach, if you are feeding them before you go leave it at least one to two hours before setting off. The best policy is to drip feed (little and often) throughout the walk.

You will probably have a first aid kit in your equipment, hopefully you or your dog won't need it but there are certain items you could add to the kit for treating your dog. Specific kits, see below, and training are available on-line.

Follow the countryside code by keeping your dog on a lead by livestock. All of these walks will bring you into contact with sheep and in some cases cattle, who can become very agitated when a dog is loose. On many of the walks there will also be ground nesting birds at certain times of the year, please consider this if your dog is off lead.

So my final words would be, do your research, give your dog the consideration it deserves, prepare your dog as you would prepare yourself and enjoy your walks.

**Harriet Bertenshaw,**
**Qualified Vet and Mountain Rescue Volunteer**

Canine First Aid Kit

NSARDA Coats

Harriet's dog Monkey

Dogs play a big part in peoples lives in many different ways, Todd may think he is "King of the Mountains" but these are the real Mountain Dogs of the British Isles, specially trained for many challenges.

You will find NSARDA qualified dogs and their handlers working with not only Mountain Rescue teams but with Lowland Rescue Teams, the Police and other Emergency Services. The dogs and their handlers provide this service completely free of charge and depend entirely on public donations.

These dogs need equipment, training and maintaining to be ready for when they are called on, please visit the website and donate to help these dogs in their work,

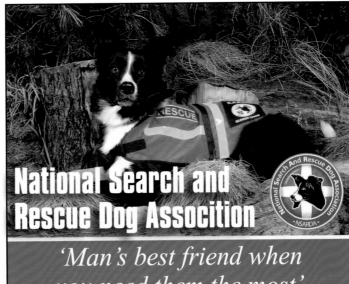

# National Search and Rescue Dog Assocition

## 'Man's best friend when you need them the most'

NSARDA have over 100 specially trained dogs and handlers on standby 24/7/365 to search urban, rural, wild and remote locations for missing persons such as hill walkers, climbers, the elderly and confused persons suffering from Alzheimer's or Dementia, those that are despondent, children and sometimes victims of crime.

www.nsarda.org.uk
fundraising@nsarda.org.uk

Registered Charity 1069110

any donation is gratefully received, you can even make specific purchases if you wish, for example:

- **FIRST AID KITS £10 EACH** • **WARM COATS £26 EACH** • **COOL COATS £71 EACH**
(Prices at time of publication)

**To donate to NSARDA please visit the website HYPERLINK "http://www.nsarda.org.uk" www.nsarda.org.uk and search for "Charitycheckout".**

**Todd is really impressed with these dogs and has decided to donate £1.00 from each copy of his book that is sold.**

# ANELU
# AIM HIGHER

**SGILIAU MYNYDDA**
**MOUNTAINEERING SKILLS**

## Mountain safety

Outdoor activities offer elements of adventure and accomplishment and as this book aims to enlighten the reader to walking routes that are achievable with a four legged friend, we should incorporate this fact into our planning stage before venturing into the outdoors.

There is plenty of information and many resources dedicated to mountain safety. However, this chapter serves only to highlight the topics we should think about as part of our planning process and is not designed as a failsafe or definitive list.

We are responsible for our own actions and as such should make every attempt to plan our activities so that we are able to have a safe and enjoyable day. Risk can never be fully removed from the outdoors but by planning well, gaining experience through suitable skills courses or in the company of more experienced people, we should be able to lessen the risk so that our day is a safer one.

Good planning for a mountain walk must consider the following factors as a minimum:

## Weather

An internet search will quickly give you access to numerous weather forecasts. However, it is beneficial to look for forecasts that cover the mountain areas of the UK. The weather found on the higher peaks can be much more challenging and should be treated with the utmost respect. Whilst we do not suggest any weather forecast is above another the following two sources are recommended as starting points:

**www.mwis.org.uk**        **www.metoffice.gov.uk**

## Route

The walks contained in this book will offer a variety of terrain. As part of our planning process we should consider the following:

Are we physically able to complete the route?

Have we the necessary skills and ability to manage the terrain and challenges along the route?

Is the route suitable for our four legged companion?

Can we navigate using a map and compass to a sufficient standard to complete the route safely?

Can we incorporate alternatives or changes to the route so that we can change our plans if needs be?

Are we accessing and passing through private land via a designated pathway or is it open access land?

Does our route have the potential to encounter farm animals, in particular cattle or sheep?

Are there diversions or restrictions in place?

## Equipment and clothing

As with all walks or activities in the outdoors, we should always wear and carry the basics. There are many sources of information for what to wear and carry but the basics should include:

Suitable clothing preferably within a layering system, waterproof trousers and jacket, hat, gloves, sufficient food and drink, extra warm jacket or top, suitable footwear and a suitable rucksack. To this list we could also add a map and compass, whistle, fully charged mobile phone, a foil or lightweight emergency blanket, a group or emergency shelter, small first aid box and head torch with fresh batteries. The above list is certainly not exhaustive and can be adapted to suit the individual. The weather and season will also have a bearing on our clothing and equipment.

Consideration should also be given to our four legged companions. Perhaps a rain cover/ jacket, over shoes or boots, food and drink, spare lead and sufficient poop bags.

## People

People are too often neglected in the planning process. Factor in enough time to complete your journey based on your ability. We need to consider the least able member of a group – this could be anyone from a person who has recently overcome an illness and is returning to the outdoors, to someone who isn't a regular walker and is taking their first venture into the mountains or our four legged companion who perhaps is not used to walking for sustained periods over rocky, steep terrain. In short – think of others as part of your planning process to ensure that everyone has a better, safer and more enjoyable day in the outdoors.

## Emergency information

Be sure to leave information about your route or activity with a reliable person at home and inform them when you have returned safely off the mountain.

If you genuinely require emergency assistance on the mountains of the UK then contact the emergency services using the following process:

## Phone 999 - Ask for the Police

After providing the necessary information they will give you instructions on what to do.

A fully charged mobile phone is now considered a positive resource in the outdoors.

Whilst mapping software and technology has improved greatly in recent years, the essential skill of being able to use a map and compass to navigate effectively is still very important.

## Other things to consider

Litter – don't leave any! Take any litter you have home with you and dispose of it in a responsible manner.

Respect - access permissions, restrictions or instructions.

Parking – be considerate, use approved car parks, use public transport as part of your journey.

Local – shop and stay local, learn the Welsh names for the peaks you are walking, check the websites of the National Park Authorities and the relevant County Council for up to date information.

## Summary

This chapter serves to help the reader to plan a safer day in the outdoors and does not remove the need for individuals to understand that activities in the outdoors carry a level of risk but by planning well, gaining experience and building on one's personal skills, the hope is that everyone's day in the outdoors will be safer one.

**Stephen Jones, Anelu Aim Higher**
**www.mountain-hill-courses.co.uk**
February 2020

The motivation behind Anelu Aim Higher is to provide safe, professional, and friendly activities. Stephen is passionate about providing people with quality experiences and believes that the outdoors should offer opportunities for all while respecting our environment, our communities, and the beautiful areas available to us. Mountains have been a part of Stephen's life for over 25 years. His experiences have led him from his hometown of Bethesda in North Wales to the Swiss and French Alps, Norway, Romania, other parts of Europe and further afield including Central America. A qualified Summer and Winter Mountain Leader as well as a former Military Ski Instructor through a career in the Royal Marines, Stephen has a wealth of experience. As a qualified Rock-Climbing Instructor, Stephen can offer a variety of indoor and outdoor climbing experiences. All staff working for the company are experienced, qualified, insured and have a First Aid qualification. Anelu Aim Higher is an authorised provider under the Adventure Activity Licensing Service (AALS), which allows us to offer adventurous activities to under 18s including schools, youth groups, scout groups and families. We offer navigation, hill and mountain skills courses as well as guided walks and events.

# THE WALKS

# MOELWYNION

*Summit:*     Moel Siabod 2861'

*Time:*     4 - 5 hours

*Distance:*     5 - 7 miles

*Maps:*     Harvey Superwalker (Snowdonia North), O/S Explorer OL17/OL18

*Refreshments:* There is a café at your starting point (not always open) and other cafes and pubs in Capel Curig, see comments after picture 13. No public toilets.

*Parking:*     A free car park on the A5 as you approach Capel Curig at the Bryn Glo Café SH.737 570

*Description:*     As you approach Betws y Coed from the east, just past the Silver Fountain Pub look across to your left to see the sharp outline of a mountain that looks unwalkable from this view, it is Moel Siabod. This is one of my favourite walks, it has it all. Gentle approach across open land, old quarry workings, wet ground to negotiate, remote lakes, mild scrambling up a stunning ridge and a fine summit with a view into the Snowdon Horseshoe worth the walk alone.

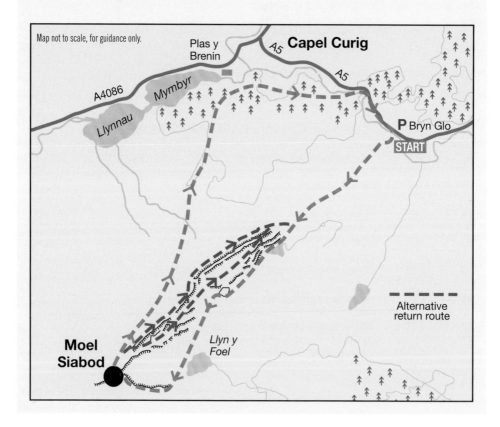

**1.** Leave the car park and turn right up the A5 for a short distance before turning left by some white cottages to cross the bridge.

**4.** Climb over the stile by Siabod Cottages and head onto open moor land. Moel Siabod soon comes into view, this is not the highest point, the summit is hidden further back.

**2.** Ignore the first track on your right and take the tarmac lane over the cattle grid. The lane winds steeply uphill gaining height quickly.

**5.** Continue over the stile towards the mountain to reach a 2nd gate in the track. Notice a stile to your right with a gully going up the mountain directly behind it, this is the way you will return if you choose the ridge route. Carry on through the gate and then climb towards the old quarry.

**3.** At a sharp bend leave the track and follow the path which by passes private property. This detour was formed many years ago after several disputes about passing through the farm yard.

**6.** Eventually you reach the old quarry pool, a beautiful setting, remember the miners that used to live in places like this. The path goes to the left of the pool and crosses above the quarry walls. In wet conditions this path becomes a small stream. Keep following it until the ground levels out and Llyn-y-Foel comes into view.

**7.** Look straight ahead to the foot of Daear Ddu Ridge to see a pathway slanting across to the left, that is your target. Easier said than done, this area can get extremely wet and although the path looks directly ahead you may have to pick your way around several boggy patches.

**8.** When you finally reach the far side, after a short distance, turn right up through a small boulder field. This is the start of the Daear Ddu ridge which will lead straight to the summit. There are many faint paths to follow, but basically if you keep to the right of the ridge that is your best bet and most interesting route with good views down into Cwm Foel with lots of minor rocky steps to negotiate. Easier ground can always be found to your left but don't stray too far or you will end up away from the summit.

**9.** Todd on the summit trig point looking into the Snowdon Horseshoe, fantastic views from here. Near to the trig point is a large shelter, a nice place for a breather.

Leave the summit shelter and head over to the edge to get good views of the ridge you have just come up.

**10.** Then turn left and head for the long ridge directly ahead. You now need to make a choice of your route down. You can follow the crest of this ridge with fantastic views down to your right of your inward route, and watch people below trying to pick their way across the wet area, or follow a faint path to the left of the ridge.

Both end up on a grassy path which leads down to the two stiles and track that are mentioned earlier in the walk, and then retrace your steps back to the car.

*Note: the long ridge can be difficult in places, but it is an enjoyable stretch and the quickest way down. The lower sections of this route can also be extremely wet.*

**11.** Todd has chosen a third route of descent on the slopes of the mountain leading down towards Llynau Mymbyr. This is a gentler but longer route home. The path is easy to follow as it slants down over grass, shale and rocky outcrops. There are wonderful views all the way down. The forestry shown lower down has been butchered over the years with little sign of it being replaced.

**12.** After crossing four stiles you eventually reach a forest track, turn left and then immediately right down through the woods to reach the outdoor centre at Plas y Brenin. Turn right along the forest road, go straight on at a large gate and follow the road around a sharp left hand bend to reach the A5 by the Siabod Café. Turn right and follow the A5 for a few hundred metres back to the Bryn Glo car park

**13.** On the way to Bryn Glo you pass the Tyn-y-Coed pub, worth a visit for a well earned pint in the garden with a stunning view of where you have been. If you have followed the ridge route back, when you reach the A5 turn left to reach this venue.

# GLYDERAU

*Summits:* Glyder Fach 3249', Glyder Fawr 3279'

*Time:* 4 – 6 hours

*Distance:* 6 - 7 miles

*Maps:* Harvey Superwalker (Snowdonia North), O/S Explorer OL17

*Refreshments:* Pen y Gwryd Hotel near your starting point and Pen y Pass on your way back. There are public toilets at Pen y Pass

*Parking:* There are several parking bays on the A4086 and the A498 in the vicinity of the Pen y Gwryd Hotel. Ref SH 655 559. Some of these are pay and display. If you park outside of the bays you will probably get a parking ticket, especially at weekends.

*Description:* The summit plateau of the Glyders is a rough and rocky place that has fantastic views all around with huge drops and steep approaches on the Northern side, however, both the approach and descent on this route, although wet in places at times, will give you easier and quieter walk than many of the other approaches to these popular summits. Once on the plateau you are unlikely to be on your own.

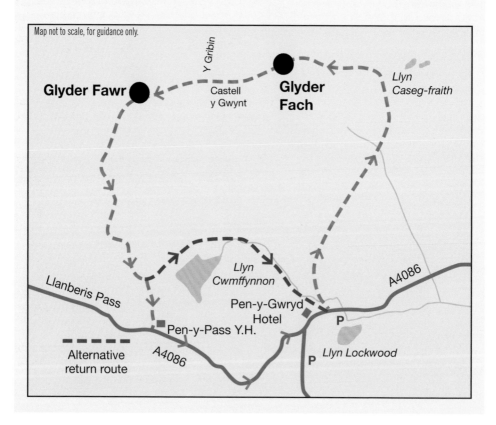

Map not to scale, for guidance only.

Y Gribin

Glyder Fawr

Castell y Gwynt

Glyder Fach

Llyn Caseg-fraith

Llanberis Pass

Llyn Cwmffynnon

Pen-y-Gwryd Hotel

Pen-y-Pass Y.H.

A4086

A4086

P

Llyn Lockwood

P

Alternative return route

**1.** Cross the stile to the right of the Pen y Gwryd Hotel.

**2.** Go over a metal bridge and head for the wall sloping up the hillside directly in front. Depending on recent weather conditions all this lower area can be extremely wet and you may have to pick your route carefully.

**3.** Once by the wall you will find several gaps in it, there is a path both sides and either will do as you begin to climb.

**4.** Eventually as the wall levels out and slopes away to the right you will come to a stile with a large prominent boulder above you on the hillside. This is where you leave the wall and follow the well worn path uphill.

**5.** After crossing a stream below a small waterfall the ground levels out with two outcrops in front of you.

**6.** You can either turn left before the outcrops or continue between them to see Tryfan directly ahead and then bear left.

**7.** Both these paths will lead you to a cairn with Llyn Caseg-Fraith on your right where you again turn left and follow the well worn stony path up on to the Glyders.

**10.** You can skirt Glyder Fach on either side as you head for Castell y Gwynt (Castle of the winds). This rocky formation has a magnificent view of Snowdon behind it and looks really spectacular when covered in snow. To go over it with a dog is not easy and there is no way to go around it on the right. Your best option is a path going around to your left and pick your way through the boulders to the other side.

**8.** After negotiating a few rocky steps you are on the summit plateau with Bristly Ridge coming up from your right. Follow the cairns to your left and after a short distance look out for the famous Cantilever on your left.

**9.** As you leave the cantilever, the summit of Glyder Fach is almost upon you. It is a rocky little climb to the summit and may be a bit awkward for your dogs legs

**11.** Eventually you will see a path sloping up the mountainside which will lead you onto a cairned and well worn path to the summit of Glyder Fawr. If you go to the cliff edge on your right there are some great views down into the Ogwen Valley

**12.** Todd having a breather on the highest point on Glyder Fawr.

**14.** Among these outcrops there are fading spots of red paint (Put there many years ago) at prominent points on the rocks. These will guide you on your way where the path becomes faint and wet in places, but it always shows itself again, and Pen y Pass is always in view below to guide you down.

**15.** The ground levels out onto a grassy area which can be very wet. The paths are the faint but visible and there is one that leads off to your left to skirt past Llyn Cwmffynnon and back to your starting point. After heavy rainfall this can be really difficult to negotiate. Your other option is to head for the large rocky outcrop in front of you where you will pick up the red dots again and a path down to your right which leads you directly to Pen y Pass. Turn left down the hill back to the Pen y Gwryd. There is a path on the other side of the wall instead of walking on the road.

**13.** As you made the approach Glyder Fawr your path home is to the left of the summit. You can clearly see the buildings at Pen y Pass below, this is your target. The scree path leads onto a grassy area which takes you to several small rocky outcrops.

# ARANS

| | |
|---|---|
| *Summits:* | Aran Benllyn 2905', Erw Ddafad Ddu 2855'<br>Other summits visited: Moel Ddu and Moel Ffenigl |
| *Time:* | 4 – 6 hours |
| *Distance:* | 7 – 8 miles |
| *Maps:* | OS Landranger 124, OS Leisure 23, Harveywalker Arans |
| *Refreshments:* | Cafes and pubs in Bala. Village shop and pub in LLanuwchllyn, public toilet in Bala. |
| *Parking:* | A free car park on the B4403 at Llanuwchllyn just before you get to the bridge SH 879297. There are limited spaces so you will need to be early. |
| *Description:* | As you travel the A494 from Bala to Dolgellau, the Aran ridge is on your left. As with a lot of other ridges it is far more gentle than it looks from a distance. The broad grassy ridge winds its way upwards at a gentle gradient with a few steeper bits here and there to reach the summit of Aran Benllyn. There are many stiles to cross and more fences than Del Boy had in Only Fools and Horses. Once underway great views are to be had all around, on your right are the Arenigs and Rhobell Fawr with the Rhinogs further back, ahead is Cadir Idris and down to your left the peaceful Cwm Croes, one option for your return walk. Two remote summits with the option of a third (Aran Fawddwy) make this an energetic but rewarding day out. |

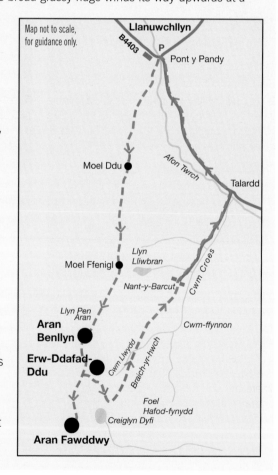

**1.** Turn left out of the car park and go through the gate at the side of the bridge.

**4.** Cross and re-cross two step stiles by an old wall keeping the fence on your right.

**2.** Follow the track uphill to reach a double gate clearly marked 'Aran', this path will take you across open land to reach another double gate, ignore a stile on your left.

**5.** After a steeper section the path meanders and splits away from the wall through some outcrops to aim for a ladder stile in the distance.

**3.** At the next gate the first sight of the Aran's is made, the summit of Benllyn is out of view. There are several grassy paths at this point and all will take you to the same place. The best path will keep you close to the fence but can be wet in places while the short detours to the left will get you on minor summits and give views down into Cwm Croes.

**6.** Getting closer now with the target clear ahead.

**7.** Soon you will climb a short steep loose section and as the ground levels out cross over a ladder stile on your left. Going up through the rocks brings you out onto the minor top of Moel Ffenigl, once again overlooking one of your routes home, as you pass a pool on your right, ignore the stiles, and keep the fence on your right as you near Aran Benllyn.

**10.** After a short stretch with the fence now on your left, cross another stile and continue uphill

**8.** Todd on Aran Benllyn doing a bit of sheep watching, directly behind him in the distance is Aran Fawddwy.

**11.** You will soon reach the poorly cairned and questionable summit of Erw Ddafad Ddu, with the towering Aran Fawddwy clearly in view in the distance.

**9.** Leave the summit and cross the stile down to your right.

**12.** A short way further on you come to a proper cairn overlooking Creiglyn Dyfi, this spot alone is worth the walk.

*Note: You have a choice here of either:*
*A. Retracing your steps back to the start, this is your quickest return.*

*B. Continue on to Aran Fawddwy and then retrace your steps (the path is clear and easy to follow and includes a short easy scramble).*

*C. Follow our return route through Cwm Croes, this is a long but pleasant walk which may bring you into confrontation with cattle and farmyard dogs. There are also several cattle grids to negotiate.*

**14.** Todd enjoyed his lunch here with Aran Fawddwy behind him. Just to the right of this rocky table is your path home. Instead of climbing onto Foel Hafod-Fynyyd, look for the path which goes directly down into Cwm Croes. Easier going for tired legs.

**13.** Your target now is the lake below the cairn. Walk back along the grassy edge for about 100 – 150 metres to locate a faint path heading down hill, use the scarred hillside opposite as a guide. This eventually bears right straight down to the lake.

**15.** You can clearly see the farm track in the valley below which will take you back to the start. It is long but easy to follow and passes through two farmyards to eventually reach a minor road. Turn left and the road takes you all the way to back Llanuwchllyn.

# THE BERWYNS

**Summits:** Moel Sych 2714', Cadair Berwyn 2724' and Cadair Bronwen 2559'

**Time:** 4 – 5 hours

**Distance:** 6 - 7 miles

**Maps:** OS Landranger 125, OS Explorer 239 and 255

**Refreshments:** There is a café and toilets at your starting point with pubs and shops in Llanrhaeadr-yn-Mochnant.

**Parking:** Follow the B4396 from near Oswestry to the village of Llanrhaeadr yn Mochnant. Turn right at the sign (To the Falls) up a narrow lane. There is free parking on the left at the end of this lane but it is not very car friendly. You are better to pay £4 for the café car park, limited spaces so get there early. Ref: SJ076 293.

**Description:** A long steady walk up the valley to the hidden lake of Lynn Lluncaws followed by a steep climb onto the Berwyn Ridge. Then an easy out and back walk, with fine views all around, to Cadair Bronwen followed by a steep grassy descent from Moel Sych back to your starting point and a possible visit to the top and bottom of the highest waterfall in Britain outside of Scotland. One of the walks in the book that is not totally circular but such is the scenery you won't even notice youv'e been on the same path twice.

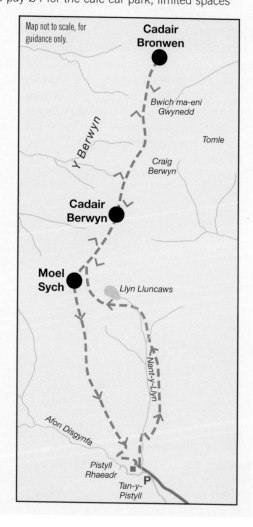

Map not to scale, for guidance only.

Cadair Bronwen

Bwlch ma-eni Gwynedd

Tomle

Y Berwyn

Craig Berwyn

Cadair Berwyn

Moel Sych

Llyn Lluncaws

Nant-y-Llyn

Afon Disgynfa

Pistyll Rhaeadr

Tan-y-Pistyll

P

**1.** Go through the gate to the right of the toilet block and climb the short path through a small wood. Go through a turnstile onto a wide track.

**2.** Ignore the rising path on your left and continue on the wider track. Your aim is for the clearly visible path on the other side of the stream. This is reached by crossing a small bridge a little further on.

**3.** Cross the bridge and climb diagonally through the bracken to reach a wide path. Turn left here and begin your climb towards Cadair Berwyn which soon comes into view.

**4.** As the track splits, take the higher route to gradually gain height along the valley.

**5.** After a few twists and turns you come to a stony area where you have to cross the outflow from Llyn Lluncaws. The path is clearly visible on the other side but this area gets very wet at certain times of the year, there are many places to cross so get ready for some wet boots while you find the best one. The path takes you past the peaceful Llyn Lluncaws, a classic setting and then steeply up on to the Berwyn Ridge with stunning views back down to the lake as you gain height.

**6.** As the path levels out the twin summits of Cadair Berwyn comes into view. Ignore any paths on your left and head straight for the peak ahead of you which is well worth a clamber over when you get there. A short distance away is a shelter, a pleasant place for a rest either now or on the way back. Another short walk will take you to Cadair Berwyn's highest point.

**9.** Cross the fence and continue along the man made walkway. This path will take you directly to the summit of Cadair Bronwen. There is a short up and down section here and the whole area can be very wet at times.

**7.** Todd on Cadair Berwyn's Trig point with the shelter and first summit behind him and Moel Sych to the right which you will visit on your way home.

**10.** Cadair Bronwen's summit with views towards Snowdonia. Retrace your steps from here and head back towards Cadair Berwyn.

**8.** Leave the Trig point and head across the grassy ridge with Cadair Bronwen visible in the distance. The path is clear and easy to follow. This is the start of the out and back section of the walk. Grand views down to your right and virtually no height loss until you reach a fence line with a boarded walkway on the other side. This was constructed to overcome wet ground.

**11.** As you pass the Trig point and head for the shelter take the path that bears right and follow the fence line for a while to cross the stile where three fences meet.

**12.** Todd on the summit of Moel Sych. Go back to the stile and bear right.

**13.** This path will take you back to the start, stay close to the fence all the way down to where it meets another fence. There used to be a stile here but it is now gone and the path leads onto open hillside, stay with it, it is easy to follow and as you reach a small wooded area take a wider track to your left and continue downhill back to the car park. Before going left, just ahead of you is a gate in a wall, this will take you to the top of the famous Pistyll Rhaeadr Waterfalls, a grand setting. The bottom of the falls can also be visited via a short path from the café.

Todd at the top and bottom of Pistyl Rhaeadr Waterfall, both worth a visit.

# BRECON BEACONS

*Summit:*      Corn Du 2864', Pen y Fan 2907' and Cribyn 2609'

*Time:*      4 – 6 hours

*Distance:*      7 - 8 miles

*Maps:*      OS 160, Altos Explorer 2 Brecon Beacons,
Harveywalker  Brecon Beacons

*Refreshments:* There are pubs, shops and toilets in Talybont on Usk. There is also a small café on the mountain road through Aber towards Merthyr as you near the turn to the Upper Neuadd reservoir.

*Parking:* Leave Talybont on Usk over the canal swing bridge and go through the small village of Aber on the mountain road towards Merthyr. Follow the road for several miles past the Talybont reservoir and climb towards the Taf Fecha Forest. Look out for a right turn on a sharp bend, signposted Upper Neuadd. Pass a car park on your right to reach other car parks on your left near the end of the tarmac road SO 032 180.

*Description:* A fantastic horseshoe walk of these three famous peaks, with an option of a fourth. A steep initial climb followed by the traverse along wide ridges giving grand views all around. After another steep pull onto Cribyn a gentle stroll down the valley takes you back to the start. This route can be exposed on a windy day and difficult in cloudy conditions but on a clear fine day it is one of the best walks in the book, no solitude here though, it's a very popular place.

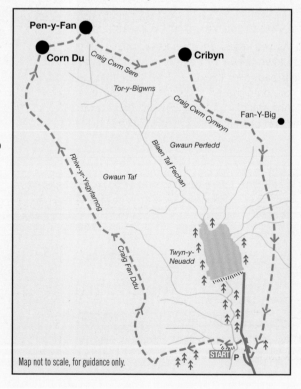

Map not to scale, for guidance only.

**1.** Leave the car park at the top end and turn left up the tarmac road. Ignore the track on your right, this is the way you will return.

**2.** As you reach an abandoned house, turn left down between some trees and follow the clear path over the dam. This leads through a gate onto the open hillside. The path now climbs steeply and the top section is worn and can be awkward during wet conditions.

**3.** As you level out onto the ridge its worth a look back at your route up from the reservoir.

**4.** Turn right along the ridge and your three targets soon come into view. This is a nice stretch of the walk with big drops to your right and fine views on both sides

**5.** Eventually you reach a junction where the path comes up from the Storey Arms on the A470. The short climb to Corn Du is right in front of you.

**6.** Todd on Corn Du looking straight ahead to Pen y Fan, this is a short and direct path.

**7.** The summit of Pen y Fan where you are likely to be surrounded by other people. Some queuing up for a photo by the cairn, and others taking in the views all around you. Whether its the Carmarthern Fans, Black Mountains or on a exceptionally clear day Cadir Idris in the north, you will not be short of something to look at from here.

**8.** Leave Pen y Fan summit here and drop steeply on the path towards Cribyn. Once again its well worth a look backwards, this time towards the face of Pen y Fan.

**9.** Eventually the path divides. The right hand path skirts Cribyn but there is no point coming this far so take a deep breath, bear left, cross the small pool and climb steeply to the summit of Cribyn

**10.** Todd washes his paws on Cribyn with Pen y Fan and Corn Du behind him.

**11.** The path from Cribyn is clear as you begin your descent back towards the reservoirs in the valley below.

**12.** Soon a distinct junction comes into view below. This is known as 'The Gap' (not nearly

as big as the gap between Wolves and Villa 2017-18). Turn right here for your gentle but tired stroll back down the valley to re-join the tarmac road just above the car park. Stay with the track all the way down, there is only one small watery crossing to negotiate.

**13.** *Note:* If you wish to make another climb for a fourth summit, continue straight over 'The Gap' to reach the summit of Fan y Big. If you have the stamina it is well worth the short climb. The summit is known as the diving board, a great photo to be had here if you are not on your own. Return to 'The Gap' turn left and head home.

# THE GLYDERAU

**Summits:** Gallt yr Ogof 2504' and Y Foel Goch 2642'

**Time:** 4 - 5 hours

**Distance:** 6 - 7 miles

**Maps:** OS 115, OS 17, Harvey Superwalker Snowdonia

**Refreshments:** There is a shop and toilet at the start point. Pubs and cafes along the A5 in Capel Curig.

**Description:** A short, sometimes wet ascent onto a wide grassy plateau, followed by nice stroll as your targets come into view. A few ups and downs as you reach the two remote summits. The route then heads downhill with brilliant views of Tryfan and Bristly Ridge and a long valley walk back to the car park surrounded by many other peaks covered in this book. Once you leave Capel Curig you won't see many people on this walk until you get back down in the valley.

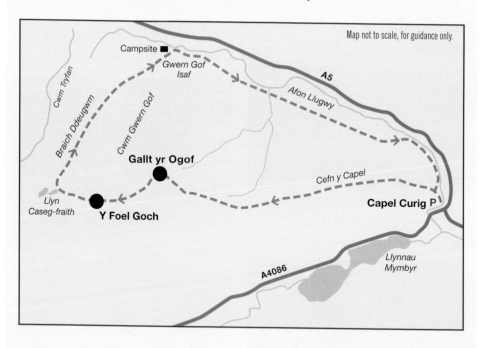

**1.** Leave the car park and turn right over the cattle grid up the track for a short distance. Cross a step stile by a gate and turn left towards a cottage, (The track in front of the gate is where you will return later), you may encounter cattle in this area.

**4.** Todd turns into a Meercat to cross a step stile in a rusty old fence. As you approach this area down to your right is the way home, a track in the valley running parallel with the A5 leads back to the car park at the end of the walk.

**2.** Almost immediately the path splits. Do not go past the cottage but take the right hand fork. The path picks its way through several rocky outcrops, wet and indistinct in places, but it always reappears to level out on a broad grassy ridge.

**5.** A ladder stile is reached as the path starts to climb. Continue uphill, steadily gaining height, with a fence on your right.

**6.** As you come to the corner of a fence the path splits, take the right hand fork and climb up the rocky outcrop.

**3.** Turn left here and follow the clear path along Cefn y Capel towards Gallt yr Ogof.

**7.** At this point, as Tryfan comes into view look out for a faint path coming behind you to the right, this will lead you to the summit of Gallt yr Ogof. You will return to this point later to continue the walk.

**10.** Todd licks his lips after a snack in the shelter.

**11.** Todd on Y Foel Goch with unrivalled views from here of Tryfan and Bristly Ridge.

**8.** Todd on Gallt yr Ogof with his first ever peak, Moel Siabod, towering above Llynau Mymbyr at Capel Curig. A wonderful viewpoint all around, but often lonely because most people aim for Tryfan when in this area.

**9.** Retrace your steps down the faint path you came on and head across the grassy saddle towards Y Foel Goch to reach a small shelter with the summit cairn to your right.

**12.** Continue downhill towards Tryfan and Bristly Ridge, this area can be very wet and there are many small paths made by people dodging boggy areas, basically you need to aim for the right hand side of the pools in the distance, a small area called 'Llyn Caseg-Fraith'.

**13.** As you reach the pools, bear right on the path down the centre of a small grassy ridge.

**14.** Keep to the ridge as best you can and don't drop into the valley on either side too quickly. Aim for the concrete road in the distance which is heading up onto the Carneddau. The path comes and goes but stay central to the ridge and you won't go far wrong. This is a great section of the walk, with Tryfan on your left, the Carneddau straight ahead and where you have just walked on your right.

**15.** As you reach the second rocky outcrop you have a choice, either stay on the broad

ridge and wind your way down among the rocks aiming for the campsite below when it comes into view or drop to the right of the outcrop onto a grassy path that hugs the ridge all the way down. The lower path is wet in places but stay close to the ridge and don't be tempted into the bog on your right.

**16.** As you get lower down the path swings right to go round another rocky outcrop to lead you to a gate and stile overlooking the campsite below, nearly down now.

**17.** Go past the farmhouse to reach the campsite and a parking area. Turn right onto the tarmac lane which leads to a track and follow this all the way back to the car park at Capel Curig. This stretch is just over 2 miles long but pleasant walking, you may encounter cattle at certain times of the year.

# THE CARNEDDAU

*Summits:* Yr Elen 3157', Foel Grach 3203', Carnedd Gwenllian 3039' and
Drosgl 2488'.
Other summits visited: Foel Ganol, Yr Aryg and Gyrn Wigau

*Time:* 6 - 7 hours

*Distance:* 8 - 9 miles

*Maps:* OS 115, OS 17, Harvey Superwalker Snowdonia North

*Refreshments:* Pubs, cafes, shops and toilets in Bethesda

*Parking:* There is a public car park in Bethesda but the best place to start
from is a small car park in Gerlan SH633 663 opposite the old post
office. Parking is limited, there may also be street parking available,
please respect the residents.
To reach Gerlan turnoff the A5 in Bethesda into Allt Penybryn ( The
road sign is not on the junction but a few metres after you turn, there
is a school sign at the junction) bear right at a fork and then straight
on over several junctions to reach the car park.

*Description:* A gentle climb into Cwm Llafar with fantastic views opening up
towards the Black Ladders and the Llech Ddu Spur below Carnedd
Dafydd, an improvised crossing of Afon Llafar (pick a good time, not
when in flood, it can be dangerous) followed by a steep climb to the
summit of Yr Elen, my favourite place of this range. After another short
climb towards Carnedd Llewelyn a stroll across a sometimes rocky
landscape to two more summits before turning left and heading down
the wide grassy ridge back to Bethesda.
One of the longest walks in the book taking in two of the most remote
summits in this range. (Note) you can easily add the summits of
Carnedd Llewelyn, Bera Bach and Bera Mawr to be included in this walk.

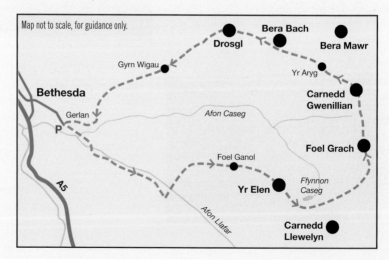

**1.** Leave the car park and head towards the school sign, shortly on your left you will pass a lane called "Ciltwllan", this will be where you return.

**2.** Keep on the main road for half a mile or so and turn left into a private road, after a few metres cross a step stile by a gate. Keep to the left of the field to cross another stile and turn right onto an old cart track with Yr Elen looming directly ahead.

**3.** Cross a stream via a stone bridge and on through a wet area.

**4.** This brings you to another ladder stile with yet more views of Yr Elen.

**5.** You are now on open ground and the path is waymarked, this area can be very wet at certain times and you may also encounter cattle in this section, continue on with Afon Llafar down on your left.

**6.** Eventually you will reach a small concrete and metal fenced enclosure, here a path heads off right towards Carnedd Dafydd but it is in this area you must cross Afon Llafar and head across the pathless grass towards the long ridge of Foel Ganol on your left.

**7.** There are shallow places to cross if you look for them, be careful when swollen, the best area to cross is just above an old dam and a small waterfall. Don't carry on too far into Cwm Llafar or it becomes more difficult to reach the ridge path you require.

**10.** Continue over Foel Ganol with Yr Elen getting closer, a steep climb lies ahead.

**8.** As you reach the ridge line turn right along the path heading over Foel Ganol towards Yr Elen

**11.** The summit of Yr Elen, with its meagre cairn overlooking a now cloudy Bethesda. If ever a summit deserved a proper cairn then this is it, magnificent views all around. The cairn is an insult to Yr Elen's position.

**9.** Todd on Foel Ganol with Bethesda behind him. As you look back your return route is over to the right above Cwm Caseg.

**12.** Todd on Yr Elen a short distance from the summit looking down the North East Ridge into Cwm Caseg.

**13.** Leave Yr Elen by the clear ridge path and head towards Carnedd Llewellyn with good views of the Black Ladders on your right and down into Cwm Caseg on your left.

**14.** After a short climb up some scree the path opens out onto a grassy shoulder of Carnedd Llewelyn,whose summit is a short detour to the right if you have time. If you are not visiting Llewelyn ignore the rocky towers on your right and keep left on the path that heads around the lip of Cwm Caseg

**15.** Eventually you reach a path coming from Carnedd Llewelyn on your right, bear left

here and head directly towards Foel Grach. To your left you have Cwm Caseg leading down to Bethesda and to your right is Cwm Eigiau leading down into the Conwy Valley.

**16.** Todd on the summit of Foel Grach with Yr Elen and Carnedd Llewellyn directly behind him.

**17.** A few metres below you will find Foel Grach's shelter, many a walker will have either rested or sought refuge in here.

**18.** A clear path leaves the shelter with two summits ahead, Foel Fras on the right and your target, Carnedd Gwenllian on the left.

**19.** Eventually the path splits into three, the centre one takes you to the summit of Carnedd Gwenllian.

**22.** Skirt Yr Aryg to the left and head for the rocky summit of Bera Bach, with Drosgl and your way home directly behind it. Note: Bera Mawr is out to your right and if you want to include it, wet pathless ground will get you there. Both Bera Bach and Bera Mawr are visited on Walk 22.

**20.** Todd on Carnedd Gwenllian, this summit used to be called Carnedd Uchaf, which ever name you use it doesn't seem like a real summit, just a cross roads in this lovely wilderness.

**23.** Skirt Bera Bach on the left, unless you wish to include the summit on this walk, and head across wet ground towards Drosgl.

**21.** Leave the summit and head for the outcrop of Yr Aryg, the path goes through a wet area but is easy to follow.

**24.** As you reach the shoulder of Drosgl a faint path heads off to the right, this will lead you directly to the summit.

**25.** Todd on Drosgl's summit, surveying his way home over Gyrn Wigau. Drosgl is visited again in Walk 22. In fact the return route from here is the outward route for Walk 22.

**28.** The path is faint in places but eventually leads to a stile over a stone wall. The quarry across the valley is now the home of Zip World, nestling below Walk 15.

**26.** Pathless at first, head directly for the minor summit of Gyrn Wigau.

**29.** Over another stile and turn left heading for some sheep pens down below

**27.** Cross directly over Wigau and follow the path with a huge quarry ahead across the valley. Ignore any paths going off to your right.

**30.** At the sheep pens turn left through a gate and follow it down hill to a tee junction, turn right and you are back in Gerlan.

# CADIR IDRIS

| | |
|---|---|
| *Summits:* | Mynydd Pencoed 2596', Penygadair 2913' and Mynydd Moel 2832' |
| *Time:* | 5 - 6 hours |
| *Distance:* | 6 - 7 miles |
| *Maps:* | OL23 Harvey Superwalker - Cadir Idris |
| *Refreshments:* | Cross Foxes Pub at the junction of A470 and A487. Toilets are available at the car park and there is a Tea Room as you enter the woods (Picture 2), this is not always open, especially out of season. |
| *Parking:* | National car park on the B4405 close to is junction with the A487. Grid Ref SH732 115 |
| *Description:* | A steep initial climb through the woods to reach the beautiful secluded Llyn Cau. Further ascent leads to a stunning ridge walk above Llyn Cau to reach the magnificent summit of Penygadair. A stroll across the plateau to Mynydd Moel with great views into the Mawddach Estuary followed by a steep descent back down to the start point. |

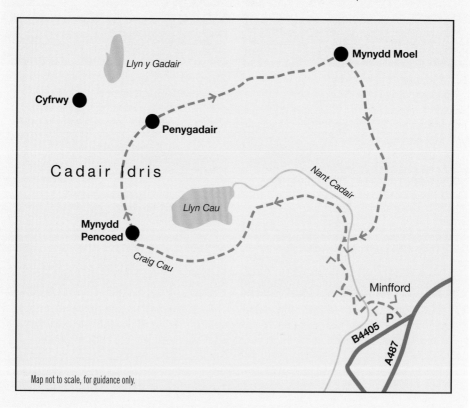

Map not to scale, for guidance only.

**1.** Leave the car park to the right of the toilets. This is a popular route and the car park fills up quickly especially at weekends, you will need to be early.

**4.** The path swings round in a left arc and Cwm Cau opens up ahead of you. Your ridge walk is directly ahead of you now with Mynyddd Pencoed to the left and Pennygadair to the right. Llyn Cau is still hidden from view.

**2.** Follow the track past the Tea Room and go through the gate on your right to enter the woods. A steep climb leads you over a stile into the open hillside. Continue to climb until you reach a fork in the path.

**5.** Ignore the smaller paths on your left until you reach a distinct split in the main path. Take the left hand path and continue to climb. (If you wish to visit Llyn Cau take the right hand path and the re-join the left hand path further on to continue the walk).

**3.** Take the left hand fork under the tree. The right hand path is where you will return and directly ahead is the long ridge which will bring you down from Mynydd Moel.

**6.** Llyn Cau soon comes into view, a beautiful setting, its worth the climb through the woods. Todd is looking where you need to go.

**7.** As the ground levels out you arrive at a large cairn, take the path to the right of the cairn and continue to climb. A few metres behind the cairn are some great views down into the valley where your walk began.

**10.** This will put you directly onto the summit of Mynydd Pencoed (This name is disputed by some). There is no cairn and this is a stunning but dangerous place. Huge drops into Cwm Cau are close by, be very careful.

**8.** Continue up hill making several short steep climbs with view points down into Llyn Cau along the way.

**11.** Leave the summit and follow the path along the edge of Cwm Cau. A steady drop down now before climbing the clear path ahead to the top of Penygadair.

**9.** Eventually you reach a scree slope on your right. (Once on a cloudy day, when Todd was just a twinkle in his Dads eye, I missed the turn at this point and ended up in the middle of the hillside). You need to climb the scree slope to a fence and go over the stile.

**12.** A little snack for Todd looking back at Mynydd Pencoed and the dangerous cliffs falling from its summit.

**13.** Continue towards Penygadair, the path is cairned in places, if you keep to the left of the rocky outcrops you will be rewarded with a fine view of Llyn y Gadair and Cyfrwy, a summit you could include now if you wish but it is visited in Walk 19.

**14.** Leave the Cyfrwy view point and make the short climb to the summit of Pennygadair. It was too windy today to lift Todd onto the trig point.

**15.** Leaving the summit you can see the shelter below and the path you need heading across the open ground towards Mynydd

Moel. The shelter is worth a visit, I bet many a tale has been told in there.

**16.** The path is cairned in places and is easy to follow. There is another path nearer to the cliffs with good views down into the estuary if you prefer that route. Ignore paths branching off to the right and continue towards Mynydd Moel.

**17.** Cross a stile and you only have a short walk to the summit. A right turn at this stile is your way home.

**18.** Todd near the summit of Mynydd Moel, spectacular views from here.

**19.** Todd by the summit shelter and cairn. Return to the stile (picture 17) and turn left to begin your decent, a long drop is ahead of you from here. The path is stoney, wet, slippy and awkward in places, take care.

**21.** A clear path appears on your right heading for the woods you started in.

**20.** There are many stiles on the way down but you need to stay on the left hand side of the fence. All the way down there are places to look back at where you have been. Keep

**22.** A little further downhill, cross the stile and make your way down towards the stream that comes all the way from Llyn Cau.

**23.** Cross the stone bridge, a great place to cool off on a warm day, turn left and go back down through the woods to the car park.

# BRECON BEACONS

*Summits:*      Waun Rydd 2524'
Other summits visited: Twyn Du and Allt Lwyd

*Time:*      4 – 5 Hours

*Distance:*      4 – 5 Miles

*Maps:*      OL 12, OS 160 & 161,
Altos Brecon Beacons

*Refreshments:* No facilities at starting point. Pubs and shops in Talybont on Usk

*Parking:*      Leave the A40 for Talybont On Usk. Turn right into the village and then left over the canal swing bridge. Just past the small village of Aber there are spaces for a few vehicles by the entrance to a pumping station. There are other parking areas a little further along this road.

*Description:* A steady climb out of the valley with views improving as you progress followed by a sometimes wet stroll with the target of Waun Rydd clearly ahead. A short brutal climb to the beautiful point of Carn Pica and on to the summit of Waun Rydd, the highest point at this end of the Beacons. An early start to this walk could see you do the entire route without meeting anyone else until your return to the valley road, real solitude if you want it. A trudge across peaty moorland until you start the steady descent to Allt Lwyd with a grand view of the reservoir and valley below to guide you back down to your starting point.

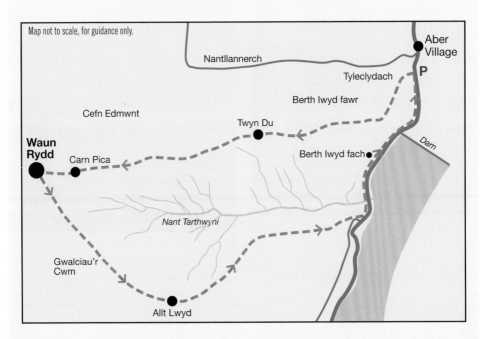

**1.** Todd at the car park, ready to go after a long drive.

**2.** Head back along the road towards Aber for approx 50metres and turn left into a lane sign posted 'To the Hill'

**3.** Climb gently until the lane swings a sharp right. At this point leave the road by a sign and grit bin and go through a gate onto a pathway, this can get overgrown at times.

**4.** Ignore a gate on your left and follow the path turning right beside a stream, sign posted 'Carn Pica'.

**5.** Pass some barns, continue uphill, cross the stream and go through a gate turning left onto the hillside by some woods.

**6.** After picking your way across a small wet area the path climbs steadily through the bracken. The path is easy to follow and as height is gained good views are to be had of where you started. It was a foggy start to Todd's walk today.

**7.** Soon the ground levels out and you are on the minor unmarked summit of Twyn Du. The huge plateau ahead of you is Waun Rydd with Carn Pica perched on its right hand corner. Wild horses are sometimes found in this area. Pick your way across the moorland, sometimes wet, looking across the valley to your left to the ridge of Allt Lwyd, this is your way down.

**8.** As you leave the wet peaty areas behind, a short steep climb brings you to the magnificent point of Carn Pica.

**9.** Continue ahead a short distance to arrive at the summit of Waun Rydd, the centre

of a flat and wet moorland. Arriving at this meagre cairn after leaving Carn Pica is like arriving at Old Trafford when you've just been to Anfield(that's for you Jim). The view behind Todd is towards The Brecon's main attractions, Corn Du, Pen y Fan and Cribyn.

**10.** Look back towards Carn Pica and take the path to the right of the one you arrived on. The path is wet but fairly clear with plenty of boot prints to guide you.

**11.** Eventually as you start to lose height you arrive at a point where the path over Allt Lwyd is clearly ahead of you.

**12.** The broad path passes the summit of Allt Lwyd on your right, the cairn here is so bad that Todd refused to be photographed on it.

**13.** The path swings left as it drops towards the forest and reservoir below. Good views of your mornings walk are to be had across the valley. Your way down is to the left of the forest.

**14.** As you reach the forest go through two gates and continue downhill. The path stays close to the trees for nearly all the way as you aim for gate in the bottom left corner of the field.

**15.** Cross the stile and follow the broad path between two fences down to the road, turn left and you have a 15 minute walk back to your car.

# CARNEDDAU

| | |
|---|---|
| *Summits:* | Pen yr Ole Wen 3210', Carnedd Dafydd 3413' and Carnedd Llewelyn 3492'<br>Other summits visited: Carnedd Fach. |
| *Time:* | 6 - 7 Hours |
| *Distance:* | 9 - 10 Miles |
| *Maps:* | OL17, OS115.<br>Harvey Superwalker Snowdonia |
| *Refreshments:* | Café and toilets at your car park by Llyn Ogwen (Recently refurbished) |
| *Parking:* | By Ogwen Cottage at the Western end of Llyn Ogwen, SH649604. there are also a number of lay-bys along the A5 in this area. |
| *Description:* | A steep but straightforward ascent to the summit of Pen yr Ole Wen with great views back down towards the A5 and your starting point. A long ridge walk over Carnedd Dafydd to Carnedd Llewelyn, with stunning scenery and a few ups and downs along the way. Followed by a gentle descent, apart from one short scrambly section, back down to the A5. A great day out taking in three of the highest summits in Snowdonia. |

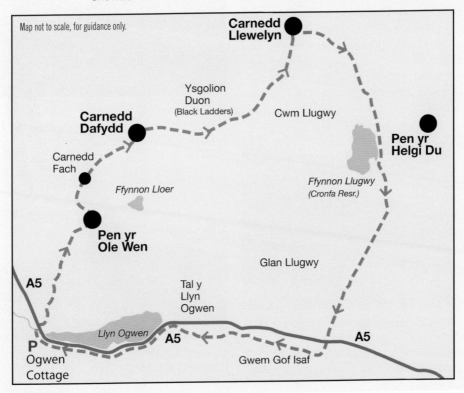

Map not to scale, for guidance only.

Carnedd Llewelyn

Ysgolion Duon (Black Ladders)

Cwm Llugwy

Carnedd Dafydd

Pen yr Helgi Du

Carnedd Fach

Ffynnon Lloer

Ffynnon Llugwy (Cronfa Resr.)

Pen yr Ole Wen

A5

Tal y Llyn Ogwen

Glan Llugwy

Llyn Ogwen

A5

A5

P Ogwen Cottage

Gwem Gof Isaf

**1.** Todd on the car park at Llyn Ogwen with Pen yr Ole Wen directly behind him.

**2.** Leave the car park and turn left down the A5. After about 100metres cross the road and go over the wall via a small opening. After negotiating a small rock step a clear path leads you steeply on your way up between the heather and rocky outcrops.

**3.** You will need to use your hands in places but the climb is easily managed and in no time at all you have great views back down to the car park with Llyn Idwal in the distance.

**4.** Time for a breather as the path levels out by a small pool and some stone steps. Above you here is a large rocky buttress with sections of scree either side of it. Both scree paths will get you up, in my opinion the left hand route is the best, with stunning views down into Nant Ffrancon as you climb.

**5.** Don't stray too far left or right but try and keep central to the ridge. As it levels out you will arrive at the summit shelter.

**6.** A short distance away across the summit plateau is the summit cairn.

**7.** A few strides away to your right is the view down into Ffynnon Loer, hiding in the valley below. Don't follow this path downhill or you will end up back on the A5 too soon. Go back past the cairn and follow the clear path around the lip of Cwm Lloer.

**10.** Todd on the summit of Carnedd Dafydd with the low cloud spoiling the views. Leave the summit and as you steadily loose height the scenery around you is magnificent. Ahead is Carnedd Llewelyn and down to your left is Cwm Llafar, home of the Llech Ddu Spur and the Black Ladders, with Yr Elen across the valley.

**8.** After crossing the minor summit of Carnedd Fach the path becomes rocky as you begin to climb, there are cairns to guide you on your way.

**11.** As you progress towards Carnedd Llewelyn the Ffynnon Llugwy Reservoir comes into view down to your right.

**9.** Soon a triple shelter is reached with the summit close by.

**12.** Another steep climb now follows on a clear winding path to the summit of Carnedd Llewelyn.

**13.** Todd on Carnedd Llewelyn looking towards the shelter. This the third highest summit in Wales and on a clear day the views are spectacular.

**16.** The rocky outcrop of Craig yr Ysfa is your next landmark, you will very often see rock climbers down to your left here. The lonely Cwm Eigiau stretches out towards the Conwy Valley.

**14.** Leave the summit on the path that is cairned directly behind the shelter. The route is clear once you begin your descent, a mostly gentle and pleasant journey.

**17.** A short scramble, care needed here, leads you down onto the short ridge of Bwlch Eryl Farchog

**15.** The path drops steeply onto a broad grassy ridge with the Ogwen Valley ahead of you and Ffynnon Llugwy down to the right, with the path back to the A5 alongside it.

**18.** As the ridge levels out take the path on your right leading down to Ffynnon Llugwy. Once the steep drop is negotiated a pleasant lakeside walk leads onto a sometimes wet grassy area.

**19.** From here you will see the concrete service road directly ahead, you may encounter cattle in this section. Follow this to the A5 looking at Tryfan all the way down. Turn right and it's about one and a half miles back to the car park.

Uncle Craig and Aunty Emm on a clear day on the Carnedd summits.

# CARNEDDAU

*Summits:*     Pen yr Helgi Du 2734' and Pen Llithrig y Wrach 2622'

*Time:*     4 – 5 Hours

*Distance:*     5 – 6 Miles

*Maps:*     Harvey Walker – Glyderau and Carneddau OL 17

*Refreshments:* Pubs and Cafes at Capel Curig. Café and toilets at Lynn Ogwen

*Parking:*     On the A5 between Capel Curig and Llyn Ogwen, there is a campsite at "Gwern Gof Isaf". There is a small car park available here. A small fee is payable at the farmhouse.

*Description:*     One of the shorter walks in the book but don't underestimate it. A long steady climb from the A5, followed by a short scramble onto Pen yr Helgi Du. A steep descent and ascent onto Pen Llithrig y Wrach, where the view down to Llyn Cowlyd is worth the walk alone. Another steep descent and a steady stroll along a water course back to your starting point. These two grassy summits are both fantastic view points and because of their close proximity to Tryfan and the high Carnedds you could well do this walk without meeting anyone. This is another of my favourite walks because of its remoteness and the view down into three mountain lakes that most people wouldn't know existed.

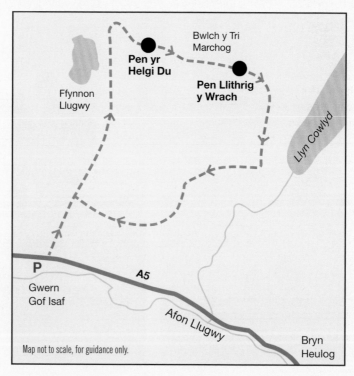

Map not to scale, for guidance only.

**1.** From the campsite turn right along the A5 and go over the stile by a metal gate onto a concrete road. (Note there are a few parking spaces here, but please don't block the gate as it is in constant use) Todd's at the gate telling me to, "Hurry up". There maybe cattle in this section.

**2.** As the road swings sharp left turn right onto a wet grassy area immediately after a small stream goes under the road.

**3.** As the grassy area levels out the Ffynnon Llugwy reservoir comes into view, a truly peaceful setting. To the right of the reservoir

a clear path is in front of you. This will lead you up onto the ridge ahead, the last section is a little steep but you are rewarded with a stunning view down into Cwm Eigiau.

**4.** Turn right and head along the ridge towards Pen yr Helgi Du. The path to the left takes you over the rock climbers haven of 'Craig yr Ysfa' and up on to Carnedd Llewelyn.

**5.** A short scramble is needed now to reach the summit, you will need to use your hands here but all is easily achieved.

**6.** Todd has a rest with the Ffynnon Llugwy reservoir below.

**7.** The summit of Pen yr Helg Du. When I told Todd this translates into 'Hill of the Black Hunting Hound' he paid his respects by cocking his leg on the Cairn. The hill behind Todd is our next target.

**10.** Worth a small climb onto the rocky outcrop here for a view down to the distant Llyn Eigiau.

**8.** Leave the summit and head off across the grassy plateau, ignore the faint path on your right or you will be heading back home.

**11.** Back onto the main path and cross the stile to begin the climb to our second summit. This climb is one of those that goes on forever, each time a small horizon appears only to reveal more hillside when you reach it.

**9.** Pick up the cairned path and drop steeply to the pass between the two summits 'Bwlch y Tri Marchog'. Wild horses are very often in this area.

**12.** At last the summit of Pen Llythrig y Wrach is reached and the wonderful view down into Llyn Cowlyd is revealed. This translates into 'The Hill of the Slippery Witch' named after a past aquaintance.

**13.** Head downhill with Capel Curig and Moel Siabod in the distance. Your target is the bridges at the right hand end of the lake.

**16.** Turn immediately right and cross the smaller bridge to join a path alongside a leat. You are about 50 minutes from the car park.

**14.** Time for lunch, a great spot, not many will have dined here. Continue downhill, the path is easy to follow until the lower slopes. It becomes wet here and indistinct in places. If you managed to stay on the path you will arrive at the two bridges. If you stray left you will end up by the lake, simply turn right and make your way to the same bridges.

**17.** Cross two step stiles, the first of many along this section of the walk, and continue along the leat with views of Tryfan and the Ogwen Valley ahead. The waterway is wide and meandering, I kept expecting a barge or a canal side pub around the next bend, it didn't happen.

**15.** There are several bridges in this area but these are the ones you need to locate. Cross over the larger bridge.

**18.** Stay with the leat as it winds its way around the contours of the hillside all the way back to the concrete road at the start of the walk. Todd's final rest of the day.

# CARNEDDAU

*Summits:* Llwytmor 2786', Foel Fras 3091' and Drum 2494'
Other summits visited: Carnedd y Ddelw, Pen Bryn Du, Yr Orsedd,
Foel Ganol, Foel Dduarth

*Time:* 5 - 6 hours

*Distance:* 7 - 8 miles

*Maps:* OL17, OS115, Harvey Super walker Snowdonia

*Refreshments:* There is a café at Abergwyngregyn and toilets at the second car park (see below) *

*Parking:* From the village of Abergwyngregyn on the A55 follow the lane Signposted 'To the Falls' Ignore the first car park and go over the bridge. Ignore right hand turn directly over the bridge.*(This goes to another car park where there is a toilet block), and continue sharp right on the lane. Follow the road to its end where there is a small parking area at the start of the walk. There are not many spaces here and you will have to be early, especially at weekends, or you will end up at one of the lower car parks and walking the lane to begin and end your day.

*Description:* A quiet start to the walk towards the secluded Llyn Anafon followed by a steep partially pathless adventure up onto Llwytmor. Another short climb onto Foel Fras before you turn for home and head for Drum. The final stretch across the five minor summits is worth all of the hard work at the start of the walk. You are more than likely to be on your own, apart from wild horses, during the first and final sections of this walk but will have company on the Carneddau Motorway around Foel Fras and Drum.

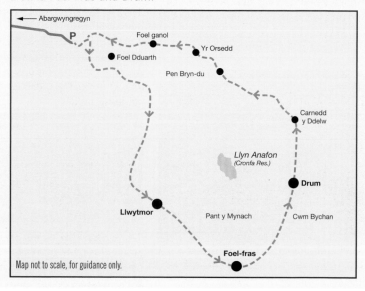

**1.** Leave the car park via main gate. Nice and calm here, it was to get windier higher up.

**2.** Pass the Carneddau stone to the right, ignore the path following the wall and follow the wide grassy path up the hillside to your left. This leads you through a gate and into the valley ahead. Keep an eye out for some stone ruins below to your right and the path slanting up the hill from that area, this is your route to Llwytmor.

**3.** A short way further on, drop to your right and cross Afon Anafon by a black pipe and onto the faint path on the opposite bank.

**4.** Follow the path until you reach the stone ruins and then turn sharp left and follow the path that runs between two large boulders up the hillside.

**5.** It is a gentle climb at this point and is easy to follow until you reach a deep gully. Cross the gully, turn right and continue uphill staying close to the gully. The path here is no more than a sheep trail and a bit higher up there is a better route in the gully itself unless it is too wet, either way follow the gully to its start point. Views begin to open up, ahead left is a rocky outcrop, do not be drawn to this, it is on the shoulder of Llwytmor and not its summit.

**6.** As the gully peters out, follow a line of boulders and aim for the ridge line ahead. Across the valley behind you the line of small peaks is your way home, and out to sea a grand view of Anglesey, The Menai Straits and Puffin Island.

**7.** Llwytmors summit cairn is perched directly in line with the path that leads to Foel Fras, Todd did well to sit here, it was so windy.

**10.** Go to the wall behind the summit and turn left. You are now on the main pathway across The Carneddau, sometimes a very busy route. As the wall ends follow the fence line downhill, eventually it swings left and levels out for a while.

**8.** The grassy path will lead you directly to Foel Fras summit.

**11.** Down to your left is the beautiful Llyn Anafon, that is where you were heading at the start of the walk before heading up Llwytmor.

**9.** Foel Fras summit, too windy today to sit Todd on trig point.

**12.** The path now climbs gently towards Drum. This section can be wet but has been recently improved by a section of stone pathway.

**13.** No summit cairn on Drum, just a gate and a shelter.

**14.** No respite from the wind today but Drum is a great viewpoint. Behind us is Foel Fras and Llwytmor with the Conwy valley the other side of the shelter.

**15.** Head off down the cart track with the final section of the walk clearly ahead. This is a wonderful end to this journey, it sounds a big order 'Five Summits' but its really just five grand viewpoints with a few up and downs in between.

**16.** After a short distance leave the track at a cairn and follow the grassy path on your right to Carnedd y Ddelw at the junction of two fences.

**17.** From here, leave the fences behind and head of down to re-join the cart track you left a short while ago.

**18.** After another short distance leave the cart track again, this time to the left onto a grassy pathway.

**19.** You will soon arrive at Pen Bryn Du, marked by a cairn of quartz rocks, someone worked hard to get these stones here.

**22.** Onto Foel Ganol with Anglesey still drawing your attention.

**20.** The path is easy to follow and a nice walk follows onto the narrow crest of Yr Orsedd with views down to your left of Llyn Anafon and where your journey began.

**23.** Drop to the col between Foel Ganol and Foel Dduarth. There is a short climb ahead onto Foel Dduarth but Todd has already spotted the car down below and was having none of it. The route now is a slanting path to the left directly behind the large boulder in the picture down to the car park.

**21.** Throughout this walk you are likely to come across the wild Carneddau horses, keep your dog close and they won't bother you.

**24.** The waterfall at Abergwyngregyn is 20 minute walk from the bottom car park.

# BLACK MOUNTAINS

*Summits:*     Pen y Gadair Fawr 2626' and Waun Fach 2662'
Other summits visited: Pen y Manllwyn

*Time:*     4 - 5 hours

*Distance:*     8 - 9 Miles

*Maps:*     OL 13, OS 161

*Refreshments:* Llanfihangel Crucorney is the nearest point for any facilities at all. Pub, Garage, and Shop all to be found here.

*Parking:*     Forestry commission car park in the Mynydd Du Forest SO 253285. Leave the A465 at Llanfihangel Crucorney and follow minor road signposted Llanthony. At Stanton turn left, signposted Forest Coalpit. At a multi-junction of minor roads take the one signposted Grwyne Fawr Reservoir, ignore the first forest car park, the car park you need is nearly at the end of the long tarmac lane at 'Blaen y Cwm'. It gets busy here mid-morning onwards, especially at weekends.

*Description:*     Another great day from a secluded location. An initial steep and tricky climb is followed by lengthy effortless stroll, with wide open spaces all around and a gradual drop back to your starting point. All the guide books I read before going on this walk warned me of "Poor Paths"," Peat Bogs", "Soggy Ridges" and even "Voracious Black Mud", especially around Waun Fach's summit.
I am pleased to say I found none of this, just a well constructed path from Pen y Gadair Fawr across Waun Fach and on past Pen y Manllwyn. The authorities are to be congratulated on the construction of this route. I am sure some sections will become wet at certain times and evidence of the old tracks through the peat is still there for you to see and be thankful you are on the new path.

Map not to scale, for guidance only.

**1.** Leave the car park at the top and re-join the tarmac lane.

**2.** Soon you pass a forest track on your right, this is where you will return at the end of the walk.

**3.** After about a quarter of a mile cross a wooden foot bridge down to your left and turn right to follow the path alongside the stream.

**4.** Cross a fence and turn sharp left uphill steeply. The first section can be wet and slippery, care is needed in this area as there is a sizeable drop down into the stream. The path is clear and although you are trapped between the gully and the forest the gradient is easy and height is soon gained.

**5.** Cross a small stream and move left to follow the fence line away from the main stream as the gully widens. Another steep section follows now but it is soon over.

**6.** A gate in the fence signals the end of the steepness. Todd's looking at the forest turning point and asking "why we couldn't get the car to here"?

**7.** Take the grassy path away from the gate leaving the fence behind.

**10.** A short break looking back at Pen y Gadair Fawr, not many places to sit around here.

**8.** This will lead you straight to the summit of Pen y Gadair Fawr. A grand viewpoint surrounded by the Black Mountains and wide open spaces. Down to your right there is a small glimpse of The Grwyne Fawr Reservoir which you will pass later in the walk.

**11.** Soon a junction is reached which is also the summit of Waun Fach.To be honest the summit could be anywhere in this vicinity and still appear lower than Pen y Gadair Fawr. It would be nice if the old trig point could be rebuilt. Turn right and follow the path towards the next summit, a pleasant section of the walk.

**9.** Leave the summit on the well constructed path with the huge spread of Waun Fach in front of you, it was once a lottery to find a path.

**12.** Todd has a breather on Pen y Manllwyn.

**13.** Leave on the clear path from Pen y Manllwyn, ignore a path going left at a small cairn and continue across the grassy saddle.

**14.** The path eventually swings right in a big arc and ends up at a cross roads just before a fence line. Turn right there and begin the long descent back to the car park.

**15.** The path, grassy to start with, becomes wet and stony in places but is easy to follow. Soon the Grwyne Fawr Reservoir comes into view, a beautiful setting.

**16.** Todd takes a look at the Dam with the vast Waun Fach behind. You may well pass a lot of people in this area who are just visiting the reservoir, it is also a track popular with cyclists. From here it is about 40 minutes back to the car.

**17.** After about 30 minutes, pass through a gate and take a look down to your right. That is the gully you went up to reach Pen y Gadair Fawr earlier in the walk.

**18.** A short walk down the road and back left into the car park.

# GLYDERAU

| | |
|---|---|
| *Summits:* | Y Garn 3108', Foel Goch 2727' |
| *Time:* | 4 - 5 hours |
| *Distance:* | 6 - 7 miles |
| *Maps:* | Harvey Superwalker, (Glyderau and Carneddau) OS 115, OL 17 |
| *Refreshments:* | Café and toilets at your car park by Llyn Ogwen (Recently refurbished) |
| *Parking:* | By Ogwen Cottage at the western end of Llyn Ogwen, SH649604. there are a number of laybys along the A5 in this area. |
| *Description:* | A gentle walk up to Llyn Idwal followed by a steep rocky climb, use of hands needed, up by the famous 'Devils Kitchen'. A brief respite by the secluded Llyn y Cwn before another steep climb onto Y Garn, one of the finest viewpoints in Snowdonia. A steep drop followed by a gentle climb takes you to the precariously positioned summit of Foel Goch. A partial return to Y Garn before a steep descent straight to the car park with magnificent views of the Ogwen valley all the way down. |

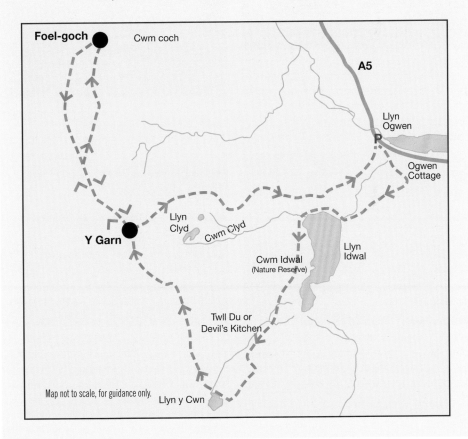

**1.** Take the path to the left of the Café.

**2.** Ignore a gully on your right, that is where you will return, and cross the wooden bridge. This is an awesome spot when the stream is in flood. Any change is welcome in the collection box a little further on.

**3.** Ignore the track on the left and swing right on to the main path all the way to Llyn Idwal. You may find cattle in this section. The path on your left will lead you towards Tryfan and the main Glyder summits. That path will be used in Walk 24.

**4.** At Llyn Idwal turn right over the bridge. There are paths slanting up to your right, these will also take you to the summit of Y Garn but that is our return route.

**5.** Our path follows the shore of Idwal around to the left and through a gate.

**6.** You are now approaching the climb to the Devil's Kitchen, which from here appears as a huge split in the cliffs above with boulders streaming from it, our path rises through those boulders. Ignore a small path on your left, this is just a low level circular walk around Idwal, and continue onwards. The path starts to steepen now, you will need to use your hands in places and it can be very slippery after rainfall. Across to your left are the Idwal slabs. A rock climber's haven, you can watch their progress as you climb yourself.

**7.** As the path briefly levels you come to a large overhanging rock with a small shelter underneath it. You need to turn right here, the other path straight ahead will take you back down to Llyn Idwal via the higher circular route.

**9.** The Devils Kitchen is directly above you now and as the path bears to the left it is worth a short detour to your right to look up the Devils Chimney, another great place after heavy rainfall. Please don't venture up the kitchen itself but return to the main path and continue upwards beneath the cliff face.

**8.** Todd looks back to Llyn Idwal and Llyn Ogwen as the steep climb gains height quickly.

**10.** Bear right to cross a stile and then negotiate a section of scree to arrive at Llyn y Cwn (The Lake of the Dog). Told Todd it was his lake but he was more interested in the sheep just out of the picture.

**11.** Bear right at the lake, and continue uphill towards Y Garn.

**12.** At a cairn the path splits, both will get you to the summit, the left fork is the more direct route, the right fork more scenic once you reach the lip of the Cwm and turn left.

**13.** Todd sits proudly on Y Garn, a place you could never get tired of visiting with the lakes of Clyd, Idwal and Ogwen below. This spot is sometimes described as the armchair.

**14.** Leave the summit via the cairned path and after a short distance, where the ground briefly levels out, locate a path a few metres to your right to look down at Llyn Clyd, this will be your route down after visiting Foel Goch.

Return to the cairned path and continue to drop steeply looking forward the fact that you will re-climb this section later. Grand views down into Nant Francon on your right.

**15.** A grassy saddle is reached where the ground levels out. Cross a small step stile in the fence on your right and then follow the fence all the way to the top of Foel Goch.

**16.** A stunning spot which looks unreachable from the two sides. The summit of Foel Goch almost takes you by surprise after the grassy stroll you just made, a dangerous place in the cloud. Todd looks down at the A5 towards Llyn Ogwen.

**17.** Another view from Foel Goch following the A5 towards Bethesda. Be careful here.

**18.** Cross the stile a few metres from the summit and drop steeply down Foel Goch's shoulder. (There are other routes down from here which would have made the route totally circular but the paths are indistinct in places and it is worth the partial re-ascent of Y Garn for the views you will have as you descend towards Llyn Ogwen.

**19.** At a T junction by a stile turn left and follow the clear grassy path. Elidir Fawr is to your right and ahead you may see an

occasional puff of smoke on the horizon. That is the train on its way up Snowdon. Todd tells me that if I ever take him on that he will leave home.

**20.** Cross over a stile to reach the grassy saddle from earlier in picture 15.

**21.** Re-ascend Y Garn to reach the route down as in picture 14, this is on your left shortly before the top of Y Garn. The top section can be a bit loose here and there but is easily managed, but the whole of this descent is a great way to end any walk.

**22.** Todd looking down to see if he can spot the car below, by Llyn Ogwen.

**24.** Cross a stile among the outcrops with Pen Yr Ole Wen (Walk 10) ahead of you, nearly home now.

**23.** After the last steep section go through a gate and follow the grassy path directly ahead with great views of Tryfan and Llyn Ogwen. The path leads over a few rocky outcrops and down through the gully behind the café and car park. This section can be wet at times and you may encounter cattle. Alternatively, after the gate you could drop down right to Llyn Idwal and re-trace your steps from the start of the walk.

**25.** The path becomes indistinct here but aim for the outflow of Llyn Ogwen to cross another stile and follow the paved path down through the gully and out by the car park.

# GLYDERAU

*Summits:* Elidir Fawr 3033', Carnedd y Filiast 2698' and Mynydd Perfedd 2698'
Other summits visited: Elider Fach

*Time:* 4-5 hours

*Distance:* 6-7 Miles

*Maps:* O/L 17 , OS 115, Harvey – Glyderau and Carnedau

*Refreshments:* There are no facilities at the start of the walk. There is a pub, café and shop in the village of Deiniolen about one mile away.

*Parking:* There are plenty of parking spaces at the end of the public road which leads to the Marchlyn Reservoirs in Cwm Marchlyn. The service road itself is only for authorised vehicles SH596631.

*Description:* A great walk for a clear day, route finding could prove difficult in cloudy conditions for some parts of this walk. A few steep and slippery sections on the way to Elidir Fawr but once that summit is reached the paths are easy to follow apart from one small section on Carnedd y Filiast. You are surrounded on three sides by all the main peaks of Snowdonia and the views are stunning. If you do this walk midweek you could spend most of the time on your own but Elidir Fawr and the service roads get very busy at weekends.

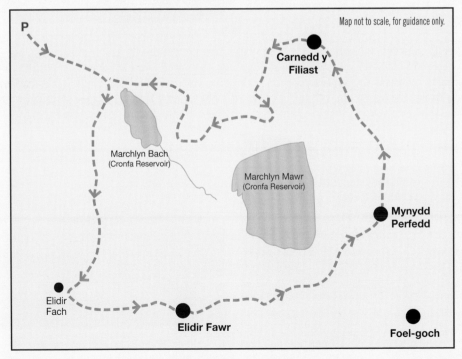

P

Map not to scale, for guidance only.

Carnedd y Filiast

Marchlyn Bach (Cronfa Reservoir)

Marchlyn Mawr (Cronfa Reservoir)

Mynydd Perfedd

Elidir Fach

Elidir Fawr

Foel-goch

1. Go through the turnstile and start your journey up the service road.

2. After passing the old Llanberris Quarry you come to a junction in the road, turn right here and the immediately left to reach a gate. Over to your left is Carrnedd y Filliast, the last summit of the day, this is where you will descend to reach the service road on your way back.

3. Go through the gate by the outflow from Marchlyn Bach and turn right on a faint path which follows the wall/fence for a short distance.

4. As the wall bears right your path swings left and begins to climb, steeply in places, towards Elidir Fach with the odd glimpse of Marchlyn Bach down to your left.

5. As the ground levels out at a rocky outcrop bear right and walk across the grassy plateau to the summit of Elidir Fach. To your left, as you walk is Elidir Fawr, you can see the faint path slanting across the scree slopes towards the summit. Todd is looking as if to say "Are we really going up there".

6. Todd on Elidir Fach with Snowdon in view across the Llanberis pass.

**7.** Leave the summit and head for the grassy area to the left of the fence.

**8.** The path up the scree slopes becomes clearer as you cross the grassy section. This could be quite difficult to find in cloudy conditions. It's not too bad as climbing scree goes but steep and slippery in places. As you gain height you get your first views of Marchlyn Mawr down to your left.

**9.** When you reach the ridge line you are rewarded with views across the valley to Y Garn and Foel Goch (Walk Number 14) with Tryfan and the Glyders behind.

**10.** Turn left and after a little bit of boulder hopping you are in the summit shelter of Elidir Fawr with grand views of both of the reservoirs, your route up, your route ahead and then your route back down.

**11.** Leave the shelter at the opposite end to which you arrived and follow the clear path which heads down towards the right hand lip of the reservoir bowl. Ignore the rocky gully on your left or you will be back down where you came from.

**12.** Todd looking across towards Mynydd Perfedd and Carnedd y Filiast, a strange choice of name when the Carneddau Range is the other side of the A5. Marchlyn Mawr below, is man made and used to drive the power station at Dinorwig. When needed, the water is released down through the mountain to produce electricity. The water can then pumped back up to refill the reservoir if required. You can sometimes see the water levels alter during the course of this walk.

**15.** After a short climb and passing a stile the now grassy path bends right towards Mynydd Perfedd.

**13.** From the edge of the reservoir the path drops sharply for a short section. From here, across the reservoir, you can clearly see the path that will bring you down from Carnedd y Filiast to reach the service road.

**16.** Cross the stile and the summit is just a few metres away.

**17.** Todd on the summit of Mynydd Perfedd looking towards Llyn Ogwen framed between Pen yr Ole Wen and Foel Goch with the A5 running between.

**14.** As the ground levels out, the path splits. Take the left hand fork over some rocky outcrops. The right hand fork will take you towards Foel Goch and Y Garn.

**18.** Todd having a breather while the shelter is being repaired by some local walkers, they were doing a fine job.

**19.** Leave Mynydd Perfedd to locate a grassy path and an easy stroll to Carnedd y Filiast.

**21.** The way down becomes clearer as a small pool comes in to view below.

**20.** The top section of Carnedd y Filiast is very bouldery, but you can clearly see your route down from in the shelter. The best path starts just to the right of the shelter before turning left to locate some easier ground.

**22.** Turn left at the small pool and begin the last stretch of your descent. At top of the small hill beyond the pool is good view down to the zip wire at Bethesda, see if you can spot the red suits.

**23.** Over the stile and through the gate before a short uphill section to reach the service road. Turn right and its downhill all the way back to the car. The climb up Elidir Fach and Fawr looks a lot easier from here now than it actually was.

**24.** Todd on the summit of Carnedd y Filiast looking back across Marchlyn Mawr to Elidir Fawr, it seems a long way now but you were there a short time ago.

# ARAN

*Summits:*  Aran Fawddwy 2970', Glasgwm 2560'
Other summits visited: Drysgol

*Time:*  6 - 7 hours

*Distance:*  9 - 10 miles

*Maps:*  OS 124, OL 23

*Refreshments:*  There are no facilities at the start of the walk, but there is a pub, shop, café and toilets in Dinas Mawddwy.

*Parking:*  Leave the A470 into Dinas Mawddwy and follow the minor road signposted Bala. At Abercywarch turn left into Cwm Cywarch and follow the lane almost to its end to find a small car park on your left. This is a free car park but there is a collection box for the Air Ambulance, please leave a donation, they deserve it.

*Description:*  One of the longest walks in the book from the remote valley Cwm Cywarch to two stunning summits. It is possible not to meet anyone on this walk despite the distance you cover. A long steady approach gets you to the fitting memorial cairn at Drws Bach, followed by a bit rougher ground to Aran Fawddwy and a long sometimes wet slog towards Glasgwm. The short steep climb up Glasgwm is tough on the legs after the long approach but you are rewarded with one of the few summits with its own lake. The last mile of descent is spectacular with your outward route and Cwm Cywarch visible down in the valley below.

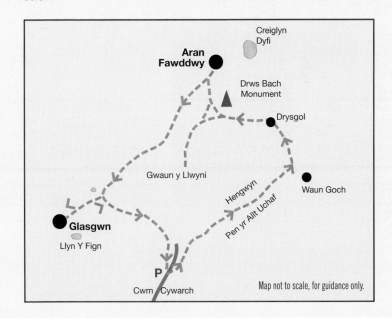

**1.** Turn right out of car park and follow the sign Aran Fawddwy. To your left is the way you will return after the walks.

**4.** The track now widens for a while and the views open up Hengwm to reveal the ridge you are heading for.

**2.** After a short distance turn left through a gate and cross the bridge to go through a small yard.

**5.** Cross a stream and ignore the gate high on your right to continue on to reach another gate.

**3.** Follow the enclosed footpath up onto the hillside. You may encounter cattle in this area. The climb up the valley is gradual but continuous apart from one short stretch.

**6.** Follow the fence for a while until the path splits, leave the fence and continue slanting uphill to your right, the path is easy to follow all the way to the ridge. On the last section of the climb look down to your left into Hengwm and pick out a compass on the ground made of stones.

**7.** As the ground levels out bear left and follow the grassy path uphill towards a stile in the fence line. (To your right is a path to the minor summit of Waun Goch, no time for that today).

**9.** Todd pays his respects at the memorial to Michael Aspain, a mountain rescue member, killed by lightning in 1960 near to this memorial, a fitting tribute.

**10.** You can do an out and back trip here to the grand viewpoint of Gwaun Yllwyni but it is some distance and Todd has already made his mind up to follow the fence towards Aran Fawddwy.

**8.** As you reach Drysgol cross the stile and continue on the path directly ahead. Now you get your first glimpse of Aran Fawddwy over to the right with Aran Benllyn further along the ridge. On your way to the memorial cairn at Drws Bach look down to your left to see the start of your walk and as you near the memorial Creiglyn Dyfi comes into view nestling below Aran Fawddwy. Todd had lunch there on walk number 3.

**11.** After a short stroll cross over a stile and bear left uphill keeping to the fence where possible. Your grassy walk just got a bit rockier.

**12.** Continue to a junction with another fence where there are two stiles. The one where Todd is lying is the one you will cross after visiting Aran Fawddwy. Bear right and continue uphill alongside the fence.

**13.** Leave the fence at another stile to cross open ground on a faint path directly to Aran Fawddwys summit.

**14.** Todd relaxing on the summit Trig Point. This is yet another great place to be on a clear day, you may well have it all to yourself.

**15.** Close by is a wonderful view down to Creiglyn Dyfi and Cwm Croes down to your left. Leave the summit the way you came and follow the fence line back to the two stiles in picture 12. You are never very far away from a fence in the Arans, if I had a fencing company I would call it Aran Fencing, I would never be short of work.

**16.** Ignore the stile on your right and cross the one directly ahead. A steep descent follows beside (surprise, surprise) yet another fence, down into possibly the wettest section of any walk in this book. It has been improved with walking boards in some areas (some of which are rotting), I would imagine that without these, after a prolonged wet spell some sections could be almost impassable.

**17.** After a boarded section the fence turns right and the path follows, Glasgwms summit cairn is calling you on.

**18.** After climbing one stile the path bears right as you near Glasgwm, leave the fence here and carry straight on past a way marker by a small pool. As the main path bears left

carry on towards a large boulder to reach another fence where you turn right and follow a faint path to step stile.

**19.** Cross the step stile, turn left and drag those weary legs uphill once again keeping close to the fence. It's a short climb but steep in places.

**20.** After crossing one stile you reach the splendid cairn on Glasgwm's summit over looking its own lake, a rarity in itself at this height, Lyn y Fign. Glasgwm has great views in all directions.

**21.** Re-trace your steps down Glasgwm and cross the step stile. Continue straight on along the faint path by the fence passing the large boulder on your left to re-join the main path down to Cwm Cywarch.

**23.** Lower down there are bits of path everywhere crossing the streams. You need to aim for the bridge below and end up on the right bank of the main stream. Todd is seen leaving the bridge, it is a straightforward path from here down through the bracken.

**22.** The final descent is in spectacular surroundings, especially after a wet spell, but the path is an ankle breaker if ever I saw one, tread carefully.

**24.** Cross a stile to join a track and turn right, the car park is a few hundred meters away past the farmhouse, the path is way marked.

The memorial plaque to Michael Robert Aspain at Drws Bach.

# Walk 17

# EIFIONYDD

**Summits:** Moel Hebog 2569'
Other summits visited. Moel yr Ogof, Moel Lefn

**Time:** 5 - 6 hours

**Distance:** 7 - 8 miles

**Maps:** OS115 OL17 Harveys Snowdonia West.

**Refreshments:** There are shops, cafes, pubs and toilets a short walk from the car park.

**Parking:** A pay and display car park near the Goat Hotel in Beddgelert.

**Description:** A great day out begins with a long but steady climb to the summit of Moel Hebog, Guardian of Beddgelert. A popular route and most people who go there return by the way they came. Our way back is much longer and secluded, you are unlikely to meet anyone until back down in the valley, it takes in the minor summits of Moel yr Ogof and Moel Lefn, gives stunning views of the Nantlle Ridge and the Snowdon Range across the valley. A steep drop down into Beddgelert Forest and a leisurely stroll back to your car visiting the secluded lake, Llyn Llywelyn, on the way.

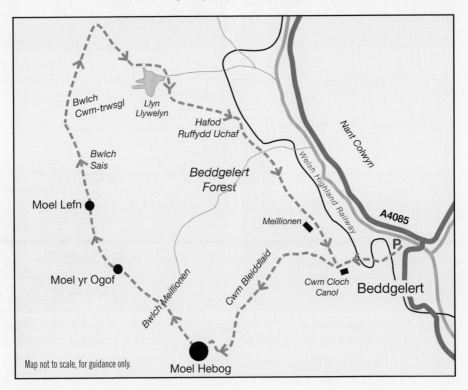

Map not to scale, for guidance only.

93

**1.** Leave the car park at the top gate, go up the path and bear right, ignore the steps and ramp to the railway to continue along the path.

**4.** Leave the main path after about 100 metres, forking left onto a paved path. Cross a small bridge and climb through the bracken on a good path.

**2.** Pass under the railway bridge to reach a lane, turn left at the Rhyd Ddu signpost. The lane climbs gently crossing the railway line twice.

**5.** The ground levels slightly at a way marked post, turn left here and head for a gate in the wall above.

**3.** As you reach a farmhouse on your left with a barn opposite go through the gate to the left of the barn, again signposted Rhyd Ddu. This is also the path you will return on at the end of the walk.

**6.** The path climbs steadily but continuously through a series of rocky outcrops and is cairned in places. There are some steep sections and very mild scrambling in places. Views behind you open up back down to

Beddgelert and across the valley to Arran and Snowdon. To the right of Beddgelert is the stunning outline of Cnicht and the Moelwyns.

**9.** As the scree peters out, a short grassy section stretch leads to a final rocky step onto Hebog's shoulder. Slant slightly right away from the drops on your left, and the summit is a short distance away.

**7.** As you reach the foot of Hebog's cliffs with Cwm Bleiddiaid down to your right the path swings left. After a short distance scramble up to your right to reach a ribbon of scree. This soon disintegrates into a mismatch of scree, path and rock winding its way upwards. Todd usually picks the best route.

**10.** Hebog's summit trig point at the junction of two walls. Not much to see today as the cloud quickly descended.

**11.** Leave the summit to the right of the Trig point and follow the wall steeply down, aiming for a sandy path between the crags in the distance (Cloud permitting).

**8.** Todd looks back down at the scree section.

**12.** Before you start the climb to the crags notice there is a path to your right here which will get you down to the forest below and back to Beddgellert if you wish to return that way.

**13.** Far better to press on through the crags over a small bridge and on to Moel y Ogof, clearly ahead on a good path.

**14.** Todd on the summit of Moel y Ogof with Hebog behind now almost cloud free. This area is very remote and it's possible you won't see anyone else until back down in the forest.

**15.** Leave Ogof, again on a good path, and drop down to cross a stile in the fence below. Moel Lefn is now just a short climb away. On a clear day the view from here and on Moel Lefn is of the Nantlle Ridge. That is a great day out but none of the summits are in the top 50 and so sadly it is not featured in this book. If you take that walk on you will need to organise transport from Nebo back to Rhyd Ddu.

**16.** Todd on Moel Lefn looking down to the forest and Beddgelert in the distance.

**17.** A stroll across Lefn's plateau leads you to a rock outcrop with Llyn y Gadair in the distance. The grassy path turns left and drops briefly to swing right above some steep drops into Cwm Pennant. Drop steeply now as your route meanders its way down. Below to your right is a forest road and Llyn Llywelyn, that is where you are heading.

**18.** Eventually you reach a wall, bear left over a step stile and continue your descent by the wall.

**19.** After a short distance as the ground levels out go through a break in the wall to

cross another stile. The path now drops to reach the forest road you saw from above. All this area used to be a stunning forest until the wood butchers got a hold of it.

**20.** At the forest track, turn left to reach a way marker, it's a wonder they didn't cut that down as well. Ignore the path on your right going over a bridge and continue on the forest track. (The path to your right will get you back to Beddgelert if you fancy a walk through the jungle. It is wet, overgrown and pathless in places, I went that way once and bumped into Bear Grylls doing some training. The forest track is a longer way back but its easy walking and you get to visit Llyn Llywelyn on the way).

**21.** At the first junction of tracks turn sharp right and head down hill. As the ground levels out, with Moel Lefn in view, turn left at the next junction.

**22.** You soon reach Llyn Llywelyn, turn right and walk over the dam and the lakes outflow, then turn left onto a forest track to reach a junction where you turn right. Todd looks over the lake, the view was much better a few years ago. Continue straight on at another junction onto a smaller pathway. Good views ahead to Arran and Snowdon over to your left.

**23.** Eventually you reach the main Rhyd Ddu to Beddgelert path where you turn right. Immedialtly after this junction there is a small gate on your right, this is where the jungle route would have bought you out. The route to Beddgelert is clearly signposted from here and will lead you straight back to the car park. You are unlikely to be on your own anymore, this path has become popular with walkers and cyclists since it was adapted a few years ago.

**24.** On the way you pass the Meillonen train station and camp site. Todd wanted to wait for the train but you are only a short distance from home now.

# MOELWYNION

| | |
|---|---|
| *Summits:* | Moelwyn Mawr 2527'<br>Other summits visited. Moelwyn Bach, Craigysgafn |
| *Time:* | 4 - 5 hours |
| *Distance:* | 6 - 7 miles |
| *Maps:* | OL17, OL18, OS115 |
| *Refreshments:* | There is a café a short distance from the car park. A portable toilet is sited on the car park but it is not always in the best condition. |
| *Parking:* | A small car park (GR 631447) in the village of Croesor, reached via a long narrow lane from the A4085 Beddgelert to Penrhyndeudraeth Road. |
| *Description:* | A long but gentle approach on the slopes of the once ravaged, but still beautiful, Cwm Croesor leads to the eerie remains of the Rhosydd Quarry. Then it's a shorter, but steep grassy ascent to the grand view point of Moelwyn Mawr. A steep drop onto Craigysgafn to look down on Llyn Stwlan and Blaenau Ffestiniog before a short climb to Moelwyn Bach. A broad grassy ridge leads you to a tarmac lane and back to Croesor. |

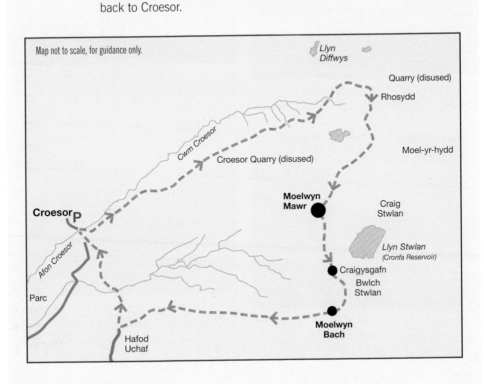

**1.** Leave the car park by the portaloo, open the door at your peril, and turn left by the café. At weekends you will need to be early as the car park soon fills up. The café is well worth a visit at the end of the walk.

**4.** At a farmhouse just before a gate, branch right onto a grassy path signposted 'Rhosydd' it is a good path and will take you all the way to the head of the valley.

**2.** The lane soon splits, take the left hand fork, you may encounter cattle in this section.

**5.** Todd gets above the early morning mist with Cnight showing itself across the valley.

**3.** Continue on even though the slate sign says 'No through road', this is to deter unauthorised vehicles heading into the valley.

**6.** The grassy path soon begins to change to get a more grey and rocky outlook with the old Croesor Quarry up to your right. As you pass old tunnels and tramways your target is the 'V' shape in the skyline ahead. This area used to be even more barren but nature is gradually reclaiming it.

**7.** A final rocky step leads you onto an old tramway where you turn right and head for Rhosydd which soon comes into view.

**10.** As the ground levels out and becomes a bit greener bear right at the ruins to climb a stile which leads to a clear path leading up Moelwyn Mawr. Over to your left is Moel yr Hydd, a grand viewpoint for another day. This area can be very wet.

**8.** At the cottages turn right and head for a rising tramway to the left of the spoil heaps. What a desolate place this is, being an ex-miner I can't help thinking about the hard graft that people put in here, probably for a pittance.

**11.** As you leave the wet area behind the small but perfectly placed Llyn Croesor comes into view down to your right. Our path goes to the left of the rocky outcrop ahead and continues to climb. Ignore all stiles and keep the fence on your left.

**9.** Todd thinks there are rabbits in there, I had a game keeping him out of the tunnel, don't be tempted in, continue uphill.

**12.** Todd takes a breather on Moelwyn Mawr

with Cnicht behind and the Snowdon Range in the background.

**13.** You can continue past the trig point and down the ridge of Moelwyn Mawr back to Croesor if you wish, but we leave the trig point slightly to the right of the path we arrived on to reach a small grassy knoll where we turn right. Craigysgafn is seen below with Moelwyn Bach behind.

**15.** A perfect spot for a break, overlooking Llyn Stwlan with Blaenau Ffestiniog in the distance.

**16.** Drop steeply from Craigysgafn aiming for the old tramway below

**14.** As the ground levels out ignore small paths to your right and start the meandering path through the rocky outcrops of Craigysgafn.

**17.** At a cairn, cross the tramway and start the short but shaley climb onto Moelwyn Bach.

**18.** Todd on Moelwyn Bach.

**20.** A look back at today's conquests, if you are ever in Porthmadog the view from the main car park of these three summits, with Cnicht to the left, is a spectacular sight.

**19.** Only one way to go from here, straight down the broad grassy ridge with views of Cardigan Bay ahead. The path leads towards a small tree plantation below. When I first saw this area a few years ago I thought the Butchers of Beddgelert had been at work here (Walk 17). It is obvious however, that the state of the forest has been caused by the wind. The authorities tell us that they need to manage the forest so why don't they clean up parts like this instead of clearing other areas, I suspect it's because there is no profit in it.

**21.** As the path levels out you reach an area which can be extremely wet at times. There is a faint path through this area and your aim is the right hand side of the wind battered forest where you will find a gate. Beyond the gate follow the path between the wall and what's left of the trees to reach a tarmac lane. Turn right and this lane will take you directly back to the car park with a lovely view of Cnicht to end your walk.

# *CADIR IDRIS*

*Summits:*  Cyfrwy
Other summits visited. Tyrrau Mawr

*Time:*  4-5 hours

*Distance:*  6-7 miles

*Maps:*  OS 124, OL23

*Refreshments:* Pubs shops and cafes in Dolgellau. There are toilets at the car park.

*Parking:*  Pay and display car park at Ty Nant, £6.00 at time of this walk. From the one way system in Dollgellau town centre, at a sign post for Twyn, branch left, signposted Cadir Idris. Follow the narrow lane for a few miles past Llyn Gwernan, the car park is on your right.

*Description:*  One of the walks in the book that is not totally circular but that takes nothing away from this day out. A gradual climb with a few steep sections, through green scenery, followed by a rocky circuit of the magnificent viewpoint of Cyfrwy. A grassy out and back stroll to the minor summit of Tyrrau Mawr to gain more grand views, this time across the Mawddach Estuary to Barmouth. The return route gives a longer option to visit Llyn Gadair nestling below Cyfrwy instead of following your outward path. There is also the opportunity as you leave Cyfrwy to visit the summit of Penygadair.

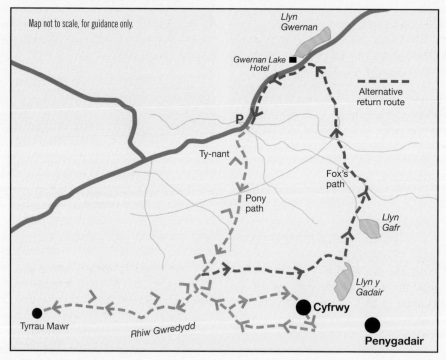

Map not to scale, for guidance only.

Llyn Gwernan

Gwernan Lake Hotel ■

Alternative return route

P

Ty-nant

Fox's path

Pony path

Llyn Gafr

Llyn y Gadair

Tyrrau Mawr

Rhiw Gwredydd

Cyfrwy

Penygadair

**1.** Turn right out of the car park. If you do this walk at a weekend make sure you are early as this car park gets very busy.

**4.** After a short while the sharp profile of Cyfrwy comes into view, it looks a long way from here, with Penygadair behind it.

**2.** After about 100 metres turn left onto a track signposted Pony path. A nice gentle stroll through a peasceful setting to start the journey. The going gets tougher later on.

**5.** Todd knows where he is going but hasn't worked out how to open the gates yet, that's why he needs me.

**3.** Ignore the farmyard track on your left and continue on to go through a gate. The well worn path begins to climb through a wooded area by a tumbling stream.

**6.** Cross a grassy section where you may encounter cattle, to pass through another gate and cross over a stream. Ignore another gate on your right and continue uphill beside a wall. The path eventually swings left away from the wall towards the zig zags on the hill side. Tyrrau Mawr is over to your right.

**7.** Todd looks back down to Ty Nant from near the top of the zig zags. This is a good spot for a rest before the rocky climb into Cyfrwy.

**8.** At twin gates and stiles turn left, Cyfrwy's shoulder is now ahead.

**9.** Walk beside the fence for a while until it turns left. We also branch left here on a faint grassy path, leaving the main path to Penygadiar behind.

**10.** As you reach a boulder field bear right to reach a line of cairns which will lead you to Cyfrwy's summit. Ignore any small tracks to your left, these lead to the top of climbing routes. It is an awkward route but it gives a circular section to this walk and is well worth the effort although it may prove difficult in low cloud.

**11.** Todd looks out of the summit shelter towards Penygadair. I believe Cyfrwy is one of the best summits in the book. The shelter is perched precariously above Llyn y Gadair, be careful in poor visibility, sharp drops are nearby.

**12.** From the shelter Todd looks down to Llyn y Gadair and Llyn Gafr, a wonderful setting. Across Llyn y Gadair you can see the ancient foxes path in the scree climbing towards Penygadair. Many text books state this route is now very dangerous, from here you can see why.

**13.** Leave the shelter and continue close to the edge towards Penygadair.

**14.** As you reach another shelter turn right to follow a line of cairns downhill. Note, turn left here if you wish to visit Penygadair's summit (Walk 8) and then return to this point.

**15.** Tyrrau Mawr is now straight ahead, the path is wide and loose in places and gets very busy at a weekend. Soon you are on old ground as you pass the fence where you left for Cyfrwy earlier to again reach the twin gates and stiles. This time we go straight on.

**16.** Time for an out and back section. Almost immediately the main path bears left. We branch right on a grassy path next to the fence. This path more or less follows the fence all the way to Tyrrau Mawr. It is soft and grassy all the way with just a few wet sections to negotiate, no waders required. This is a welcome terrain for Todd after the stony motorway we just left.

**17.** Cross the step stile on the ridge to reach the top of Tyrrau Mawr.

**19.** Here we are again at the twin gates, this time we turn left and begin our descent down the zig zags.

**18.** No summit marker to speak of but a magnificent view across Llynnau Gregennen and the Mawddach Estuary towards Barmouth. There are other routes down from here but they are indistinct and you will end up with a long tarmac march back to the car park. Much better to stay up here and re-trace our steps back towards the twin gates and stiles, Cyfrwy and Penygadair look out of reach as you head back in their direction.

**20.** At the bottom of the zig zags there is the option of another route back to the car park. Where the pony path makes its last left turn there is a faint grassy path heading off right. This will lead you to the grand setting below Cyfrwy and the twin lakes of Llyn y Gadair and Llyn Gafr. It is a wonderful spot, but will extend your walk by about another hour and the path is not the best one you will ever walk. If you go that way, the path roughly follows the bottom of the screes to reach Llyn y Gadair. Cross the outflow and descend to Llyn Gafr where you follow the Old Foxes Path back to lane by Llyn Gwernan where you turn left to reach the car park. Today though, Todd has had enough and we follow our outward route back to Ty Nant.

# SNOWDON

| | |
|---|---|
| *Summits:* | Snowdon 3561', Garnedd Ugain 3499', Y Lliwedd 2947'<br>Other summits visited Lliwedd Bach |
| *Time:* | 5-6 hours |
| *Distance:* | 6-7 miles |
| *Maps:* | OL17, Harvey – Snowdonia |
| *Refreshments:* | All facilities are at the car park at Pen y Pass and on the summit of Snowdon if the café is open, no dogs allowed! |
| *Parking:* | SH647555 Carpark at Pen y Pass Hostel on the A4086 Llanberris Road. It is £10 all day and you will have to be early, especially at weekends, you will be lucky to get a space after 6.00am. There is other parking by the Pen y Gwryd Hotel where the A4086 joins the A498, make sure you get a ticket. Traffic Wardens are looking for victims every weekend. |
| *Description:* | The Snowdon Horseshoe is widely acclaimed as one of the best mountain walks in the British Isles. This walk takes in three of the four Horseshoe summits, leaving out Crib Goch because of the unsuitable terrain for animals and possibly their owners. There are many routes up Snowdon but this, Horseshoe, in reverse direction, gives you a quiet start to the day up and over the summit of Y Lliwedd before you reach the crowds on and around Snowdon. The mountain has become too popular for its own good and if you want to get near the summit a weekday would be a better option. A visit to Garnedd Ugain, the second highest point in Wales, is easily achieved and worth it for a bit of peace and quiet for a while. The only people you meet here will have come over Crib Goch. A choice of scenic routes back finishes the walk, which despite the crowds, is spectacular throughout and well worth the effort required. |

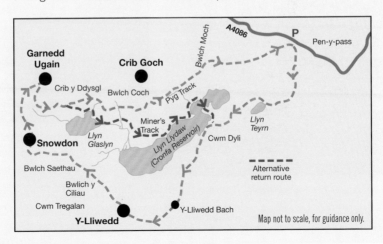

**1.** Todd and Gail leave the bottom car park on the Miners track .

**2.** Fairly quickly your route opens up in front of you, Y Lliwedd to the left, Snowdon central and Crib Goch to the right, with Garnedd Ugain out of sight.

**3.** Todd looks over the Old Miners Cottages at Llyn Teyrn.

**4.** The path forks as you reach Llyn Llydaw, take the left hand route past the pumping station.

**5.** The path follows the shore for a while, crosses a bridge and begins to climb towards Y Lliwedd Bach. Ignore any grassy paths to your right. These lead to the climbers routes on the cliffs below Y Lliwedd, the tallest cliff face in Wales.

**6.** The path degenerates a little into a section of rock steps and scree, eventually as you gain the ridge, you arrive at a cairn where you turn right.

**8.** As you approach Y Lliwedd there are great views to your left down into Nantgwynant, where the Watkin paths start from.

**7.** Y Lliwedd Bach looms in front if you wish to visit it, Todd is taking the shoulder route saving himself for better things.

**9.** Views also appear down to Llyn Llydaw down to your right with Crib Goch on the skyline above.

**10.** Todd takes a breather on Y Lliwedd, a magnificent and often quiet place, both summits are worthy of a few moments.

**11.** As you leave Y Lliwedd a clear scree path, cairned in places,winds down in front of you. There are many twists and turns to follow but don't drop too far left. Ahead of you in the distance is the path heading towards Snowdon, that is where to aim for.

**14.** Todd takes a breather before taking on the last steep section to Snowdon.

**12.** As the drop levels out for a while, over to your right you will get a great view of Y Lliwedd's cliffs, big drops in this area, be careful.

**15.** From the stone marker over to your right is a great spot above Llyn Glaslyn with the Miners and Pyg tracks behind it.

**13.** Eventually at a grassy area you will join the Watkin Path coming up from your left. This is a gentle section and the path

**16.** The first part of the climb is the worst section of this walk, loose and slippery scree everywhere. The only saving grace is the view down to the Watkin path while you take a breather. However, the top section has now been expertly paved, lets hope the rest gets done when funding allows. As you reach two stone pillars, one old, one new, you join the path coming from the south ridge and Rhyd Ddu. Turn right here and the summit is close by.

**17.** The café soon appears along with lots of people, Todd's not impressed, they won't let him in and they don't sell Bonio's.

**19.** There are many places near the summit but away from the crowds to take in the views on all sides.

**18.** Todd manages to get on the summit cairn. This was on a Tuesday. At weekends its almost impossible, due to the amount of people up there, and some selfish ones who think they own it when they get there making others wait a long time for their photo. We were lucky today and had assistance from all around.

**20.** Leave the summit area on the path adjacent to the railway, please don't walk directly on the railway track itself.

**23.** Continue on and take the right hand path climbing up towards Garnedd Ugain. The left hand fork will take you down to Lanberris and the sharp left over the railway will take you down the Snowdon Ranger path, both will leave you a long way from your car.

**21.** Todd looks down at Llyn Glaslyn and Llyn Llydaw and the way home.

**22.** Soon you reach two more stone markers, again one old, one new, your way home is down to the right, but not yet.

**24.** If ever there was a way to cheat your way to a summit then this is it. Garnedd Ugain is the second highest summit in Wales yet here it is just a few steps away from the main Snowdon routes. To earn its full respect climb it from the Llanberris Pass, but don't take Todd. Lets hope the summit trig point, framed perfectly between Y Lliwedd and Snowdon, gets a makeover one day. Don't be tempted onwards, especially if you have a dog, or you will end up on Crib Goch. This is the wrong direction to approach it from anyway. The view from here will show you what you are up against.

**25.** Return to the two stone markers and turn left to start your descent among the crowds.

**28.** Todd has his eyes on the sheep by the twin stiles that lead to the final section of the walk.

**26.** At another stone marker you have a choice of return routes, both lead to the car park at Pen y Pass. Continue straight on with Todd on the Pyg track  high level route or turn right onto the Miners path and drop down to return via the lakes which in my opinion is easier walking but always busier.

**29.** By the stiles you can look down to the causeway over Llyn Llydaw and towards the pumping station where you began your ascent of Y Lliwedd

**27.** View from the Pyg track down into Llyn Glaslyn.

**30.** After the stiles the path bends left for the final descent and gives good views down into the Llanberris Pass. Soon Pen y Pass comes into view and you are nearly home.

# CARMARTHEN FANS

*Summits:* Fan Brycheiniog 2632' Fan Hir 2494'
Other summits visited: Fan Foel, Picws Du

*Time:* 4-5 hours

*Distance:* 6-7 miles

*Maps:* OS160 OL12

*Refreshments:* There are no facilities anywhere near the start of this walk. Towns on the A40 or A4069 are your nearest options.

*Parking:* Head for Cross inn and Llanddeusant either from the A4069 Brynamman to Langadog road or from Trecastle on the A40. These roads are remote and narrow. When near Llanddeusant you will pick up signs for Blaenau and the Lake etc, from Blaenau Farm the last section is a stony track, but the parking area is clear and spacious.

*Description:* Maybe the remotest walk in the book and also one of the best, we passed no one until nearly back at the car. The gradients are mostly gentle and the paths are easy to follow throughout. Two lengthy cliff edge paths above two remote mountain lakes and on a clear day views for miles around in all directions across the wilderness below. A great day out.

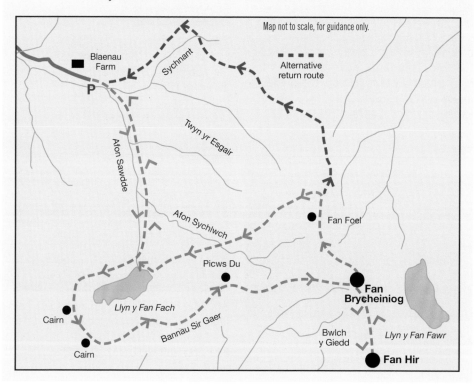

1. As you leave the car park and head up the stony access road towards Llyn y Fan Fach,the striking outline of Picws Du soon comes into view. If the barrier is down don't be tempted to drive past this point as you may become trapped.

4. Ignoring a wide grassy track on your left continue up to the lake and as you reach the outflow turn right onto a small but well defined grassy path.

2. The path detours around the pumping/outflow station to rejoin the track.

5. Todd keeps his eyes on the sheep as the path climbs gently and gradually before arcing left to reach the ridge.

3. As the gentle gradient continues the full ridge of Bannau Sir Gaer comes into view. Your last summit of the day, Fan Foel, is over to the left. Fan Brycheiniog and Fan Hir are out of sight at this point.

6. A first look back to Llyn y Fan Fach and the way ahead over Bannau Sir Gaer with Fan Foel in the distance and your route back across the moors towards the lake at the end of the walk.

**7.** Todd takes a breather on one of the pathways cairns.

**8.** A great view point from Bannau Sir Gaer to Llyn y Fan Fach and your route from the car park below.

**9.** Distance is soon eaten up on this cliff top pathway to reach the summit of Picws Du, the dominant feature throughout this walk. It's a shame this point is not in the top 50 instead of Fan Hir, you will see why when you get there.

**10.** A steeper section now follows as you leave Picws Du to drop down to the col below. Ignore the wilderness to your right and the well defined path climbing to your left and carry straight on, sharply uphill on a well defined and occasionally wet path, directly to the summit of Fan Brycheiniog

**11.** Todd on Fan Brycheiniog surveying the barren landscape below.

**12.** Close to the trig point a view opens up down to Llyn y Fan Fawr.

**13.** Leave the trig point and go past the round shelter and drop down the paved path towards Fan Hir. Ignore a path on the left going down to the lake and make the short climb to Fan Hir's summit. A great view from here to the Brecon Beacons in the distance.

**16.** A short walk past the trig point brings you to a second cairn on Fan Brycheiniog .

**14.** Retrace your footsteps back to Fan Brycheiniog with Llyn y Fan Fawr down to your right. A short climb but a necessary evil for all summit baggers.

**17.** Leave the cairn and follow the cliff top path towards Fan Feol in the distance. There is a real sense of isolation in this section due to the surrounding landscape.

**15.** Time for a snack in the well built shelter.

**18.** Pass a small tarn on your left to reach the poorly marked summit of Fan Foel, surely these prominent places deserve better decoration.

**19.** Leave Fan Foel on the central grassy path, ignoring a smaller path to your right which goes down to the lake and the well laid path which heads back to Picws Du.

**22.** Follow the path across the moorland. It is soft easy walking and not too wet considering how open the ground is.

**20.** The path drops steeply now, and as it levels out you reach a grassy crossroads just before some rocky outcrops on your left. Turn left here and follow a good path which contours around the hillside below Fan Foel.

**23.** As Llyn y Fan Fach gets closer the path bears left to cross a stream below an old dam. The path now runs beside an old leat for its final section. Ignore all the faint paths on your right and follow the leat back to the lake.

**21.** At a point where Picws Du again becomes prominent and you can see Llyn y Fan Fach in the distance look for a clear grassy path going down to your right.

**24.** Back on old ground now, turn right at the pumping station and follow the track back to the car park.

# THE CARNEDDAU

*Summits:*  Bera Bach 2648' Bera Marw 2606' Drosgl 2488'
Other summits visited: Moel Wnion, Gyrn Wigau, Gyrn, Lefn, Moel
Faban.

*Time:*  5-6 hours

*Distance:*  6-7 miles.

*Maps:*  OS115.  OL17 Harvey Superwalker Snowdonia North.

*Refreshments:* Pubs, cafes, shops and toilets in Bethesda.

*Parking:*  There is a public car park in Bethesda but the best place to start is a
small car park in Gerlan SH633 663 opposite the old post office.
Parking is limited, there may also be some street parking, please
respect the residents. To reach Gerlan turn off the A5 in Bethesda
into Allt Penybryn ( the road sign is not on the junction but a few
metres after you turn, there is a School sign at the junction), bear right
at a fork and then straight over several junctions to reach the car park.

*Description:*  A gentle but continual climb to two of the rockiest summits in the
Carneddau, Bera Mawr should be renamed Mini-Tryfan, it has its own
Cannon as well as Adam and Eve, the outward route to Bera Bach
is the return route of walk 7. This is a walk to save for a clear day,
there are some pathless sections which could prove difficult in poor
visibility. You could spend a lot of time on your own during this walk
with just the Carneddau Ponies for company. After visiting Drosgl
(also in Walk 7), a partially pathless descent leads to Moel Wnion and
then a leisurely grassy stroll back down to Bethesda. A long but great
day out in a remote area, save it for a clear day and your efforts will be
rewarded.

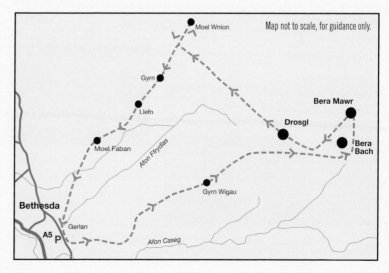

**1.** Leave the car park and head off past the school sign. This is the same car park used in Walk 7, you will benefit from an early start. The outward route as far as Drosgl is also the return route from Walk 7.

**2.** Take the first left into a tarmac lane, Ciltwllan, this soon changes into a cart track which finishes at some sheep pens. Good views over to your right of Yr Elen and Carnedd Dafydd.

**3.** At the sheep pens go through the gate and turn right.

**4.** Turn left after a few metres to pass a large boulder.

**5.** Just after the boulder ignore a path branching right by a fence and continue uphill on a broad grassy path.

**6.** Ignore a few more small paths on your right and continue uphill. The path eventually bends right to reach a stile in a fence. Soon you reach another stile in a wall with the clear path in front of you to the minor unmarked summit of Gyrn Wigau.

**7.** Once over Gyrn Wigau the route is clear towards Drosgl with Bera Bach further on in the distance. A nice grassy stroll before the rocky summits ahead,over to your left is Moel Wnion and your route back to Bethesda.

**10.** After a few rocky outcrops a grassy path skirts Bera Bach to the right, that is your way to Bera Mawr. For now leave the path and make the short scramble to Bera Bach's summit, you may have to carry your dog in places. Todd sits on Bera Bach with a great view to Yr Elen.

**8.** As you near Drosgl, ignore the summit up on your left and stay with the wide path that traverses across its shoulder.

**11.** Return to the grassy path you left and cross a small boulder field. Branch left off the main path towards Bera Mawr. Faint paths come and go in this sometimes wet area.

**9.** The path heads directly towards Bera Bach with Bera Marw coming into view over to your left. Further on are the higher Carneddau summits of Foel Fras and Foel Grach.

**12.** Head roughly towards the centre of Bera Mawr's rocky spread, look out for a cannon on the right of the summit and aim for that area.

**13.** Todd sits by the cannon and asks when is he going to Tryfan to see the real one.

**14.** Just around the corner from the cannon is Bera Mawr's own Adam and Eve, I bet nobody has jumped these. Todd looks out over Anglesey.

**15.** Leave Bera Mawr and head back towards Bera Bach but not the direction you approached from. Aim for the right of Bera Bach and locate a grassy path that hugs its base.

**16.** Continue around Bera Bach to reach the wide grassy path from earlier, bear right and after a short distance branch right again onto a smaller path to the summit of Drosgl.

**17.** Todd stands on Drosgl looking back to Bera Mawr and Bera Bach. You can head for Gyrn Wigau if you wish to re-trace your outward route and shorten your walk.

**18.** Leave Drosgl by passing what looks like a huge shelter. It is in fact a mass of stones, you could build a shelter if you had time. Continue downhill, mainly pathless but easy going and head for the small pointed summit of Gyrn.

**19.** Lower down you reach a wide track, turn right here before the track bends left and heads directly to the col between Gyrn and Moel Wnion. Ignore any paths to your right, they lead down to Abergwyngregyn and its mighty waterfalls.

**20.** At a grassy crossroads by Gyrn turn right for the short climb to Moel Wnion. A fine summit, better marked than some of its superiors, with a shelter build around the old trig point.

**21.** Return to the cross roads and climb past the sheepfolds to summit of Gyrn.

**22.** Todd looks out from Gyrn's shelter over Lefn and Moel Faban towards Bethesda.

**23.** Leave Gyrn's boulders behind and head off over the minor hill of Lefn. Paths down to your left will also take you home.

**24.** After crossing Lefn, drop steeply and bear left to avoid a deep gully. At the mouth of the gully bear right and climb up through the gorse to the summit of Moel Faban and its two shelters.

**25.** Todd on Moel Faban, with shelters behind, looks down towards Bethesda.

**26.** Leave Moel Faban on a clear path heading for Bethesda down to a turnstile by some gates.

**28.** The track soon turns into a tarmac road which will take you into Bethesda, good views on the way down of the huge zip wire below Carnedd y Filiast.

**27.** Go through the turnstile and follow the path by a wall to join a track, you may encounter cattle in this area.

**29.** Turn left at a T-junction and follow the road to a crossroads where you turn left again to reach your car after a short distance.

# ARENIG

| | |
|---|---|
| *Summits:* | Arenig Fawr 2802' |
| | Other summits visited: Y Castell |
| *Time:* | 4-5 hours |
| *Distance:* | 5-6 miles |
| *Maps:* | OL18, OS124/125 |

*Refreshments:* All facilities are in Bala, however, there are toilets and a café on the A4212 not far from Llyn Celyn.

*Parking:* Leave the A4212 near its junction with the B4391 onto a minor road signposted Arenig Llidiardau. Continue past the old quarry and look out for a small parking area (GR 845395) on your left just after passing some cottages, Pant Yr Hedydd. The path to Arenig Fawr is opposite the parking area. There are not many spaces so you will need to be early, especially at weekends. If there are no spaces you will have to park at the old quarry and walk back to the access gate.

*Description:* Although there is a circular section to this walk, the start and the end of the walk uses the same route, made worthwhile by the views down to Llyn Arenig Fawr as you return. There is an option to make it totally circular via Moel Lyfnant but this would add 4 miles to the journey and leave a long tarmac section back to your car. Easy walking throughout with gentle slopes for most of the way, this walk passes a mountain lake in a beautiful setting to reach the remote summit of Arenig Fawr with its recently renewed summit memorial. Surrounded by the Arenig moorland this walk has a feeling of remoteness and you may not see anyone else, especially mid week.

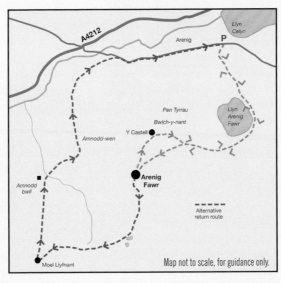

**1.** Go through access gate onto the wide track leading to Llyn Arenig Fawr.

**3.** As you near the lake the route to Arenig Fawr is the path you can see at the far end of the Dam.

**2.** It's not long before the isolated setting of the lake comes into view.

**4.** Go past a bench and take the small path heading down towards a small hut.

**5.** The old pump house is now a bothy with central heating, this was a cold October morning and Todd wanted me to light the fire.

**6.** Go over the stile by the Bothy to cross the outflow from the lake on a small makeshift bridge.

**7.** The clear path now winds it's way gently upwards, wet in places, and height is gained quickly with good views down to the lake.

**8.** It's a bit like a long staircase and no hands are required. After a steeper section the path crosses a fence via a pile of stones, Llyn Arenig Fawr soon disappears from view.

**9.** Arenig Fawr comes into view over to your left as you reach another fence.

**10.** After about 30 metres, cross the fence again via some rocks, to access the clear path on the other side. Ignore the path to the left of the fence. Considering we are fairly close to the fence and stile infested Arans you would think a couple of decent step stiles could be installed here.

**11.** Shortly there is a wet section to cross (Bwlch y Nant),higher up to the right of the wet area is Y Castell from where you will return later.

**12.** Past the wet area the grassy path starts to climb and swings left to contour the hillside for some distance. Above you is the ridge you will travel on your return.

**14.** The path now becomes a mixture of scree, grass and rocks.

**13.** After a considerable distance the terrain becomes a bit rockier and the path bears right uphill beside a cairn with a large boulder above on the hillside.

**15.** Eventually you are on the wide ridge with the summit clearly ahead. Remember this rock and small cairn if you wish to return the same way.

**16.** Todd arrives at the summit for a spot of posing and sheep watching.

IN MEMORY OF THE CREW OF THE FLYING FORTRESS
WHICH CRASHED ON THE ARENIG FAWR 4TH AUGUST 1943.
1ST LT JAMES N. PRATT. BOISE. IDAHO.
2ND LT ALLAN M. BONER. TINLEY PARK. ILLINOIS.
2ND LT WILLIAM A. BOWLING. COVINGTON. KENTUCKY.
T/SGT FREDERIC J. ROYAR. QUEENS VILLAGE, NEW YORK
S/SGT WALTER J. JOHNSTON. FAYETTE. OHIO.
SGT WALTER B. ROBINSON. SACRAMENTO. CALIFORNIA
SGT PHILLIP SIMONTE. HIGHLAND PARK. MICHIGAN.
PTE ALFRED B. VAN DYKE. BROOKVILLE, PENNSYLVANIA

**17.** Todd on the trig point, still not smiling and still too interested in the sheep.

IN MEMORY OF THE CREW OF THE FLYING FORTRESS
WHICH CRASHED ON THE ARENIG FAWR 4TH AUGUST 1943.
1ST LT JAMES N. PRATT. BOISE. IDAHO.
2ND LT ALLAN M. BONER. TINLEY PARK. ILLINOIS.
2ND LT WILLIAM A. BOWLING. COVINGTON. KENTUCKY.
T/SGT FREDERIC J. ROYAR. QUEENS VILLAGE. NEW YORK
S/SGT WALTER J. JOHNSTON. FAYETTE. OHIO.
SGT WALTER B. ROBINSON. SACRAMENTO. CALIFORNIA.
SGT PHILLIP SIMONTE. HIGHLAND PARK. MICHIGAN.
PFC ALFRED B. VAN DYKE. BROOKVILLE. PENNSYLVANIA.

**18.** The newly refurbished memorial to the crew of a Flying Fortress which crashed in 1943.

**19.** Just beyond the summit is the view to Arenig Fawr's second top and Moel Lyfnant. That walk is a great secluded journey and is well documented in many other books, but that is not for Todd today.

**20.** Leave the summit by the way you came and drop back down to the broad ridge. At some white quartz rocks head across the ridge towards some fence posts.

131

**21.** At the second fence post follow the faint grassy path slanting down to your right towards some rocky outcrops. You are now running parallel above your route from earlier on.

**23.** As Llyn Arenig Fawr comes clearly into view, bear right down the hillside by a rocky area and pick up a small path leading back up onto Y Castell keeping a large gully to your left. Don't go too far towards the lake or you will eventually end up on poor terrain.

**22.** Continue on a bit further with the wet area of Bwlch y Nant down to your right, your aim is the rocky crest of Y Castell sitting above it.

**24.** A great view from Y Castell over Llyn Arenig Fawr to Lynn Celyn. From this point, walk away from the cliffs, across the grass for a short distance to reach your outwards path at Bwlch y Nant. Turn left and enjoy the views all the way back down to Llyn Arenig Fawr. Maybe find some time to sit on the bench by the Dam, a great place for a snack before you return to your car.

# GLYDERAU

*Summits:*      Tryfan

*Time:*      3-4 hours

*Distance:*      3-4 miles

*Maps:*      Harvey Superwalker, Glyderau and Carneddau, OL17

*Refreshments:* Café and toilets at your car park by Llyn Ogwen.

*Parking:*      Car park by Ogwen Cottage at the western end of Llyn Ogwen, there are also several laybys along the A5 in this area.

*Description:*      The shortest walk in the book but certainly not the easiest, you will need to use your hands at some point during this climb and give your dog a bit of assistance here and there on one of Snowdonia's most iconic Mountains. The North Ridge is the classic way to Tryfan's summit passing the famous "Cannon" on the way, but I believe this route is not suitable to travel with your dog. There are a few awkward bits to negotiate and with all the gullies around mistakes can easily be made, many people each year are rescued along this route, usually in descent. So the route we have chosen takes you from Llyn Ogwen up to Llyn Bochlwyd before cutting across to a notch in the South Ridge. From here a steep scramble leads to the magnificent summit of Tryfan with its twin towers of Adam and Eve, well worth the effort. The return is via either the spacious Heather Terrace or the lonely Cwm Tryfan and then a gentle stroll down the A5 past Llyn Ogwen.

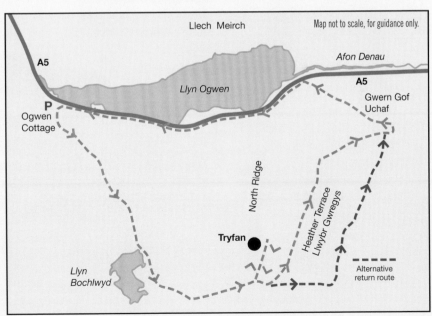

**1.** Take the path to the left of the Café, ignore a gully on your right, to reach a footbridge.

**2.** Cross the bridge, a lovely spot when the water is in full flow, don't forget to put a donation in the collection box. Tryfan stands dead ahead with Bristly Ridge to the right leading upon to the Glyders.

**3.** As the main path bends right towards Llyn Idwal and the Devils Kitchen, Walk 14, take the smaller path on the left and head for the right hand side of the waterfall in the distance.

**4.** You may encounter Cattle and Wild Horses in this area as you approach the waterfall.

**5.** The path is steep but not difficult apart from one short wet section. As the path levels out ignore the branch going right and cross the outflow from Llyn Bochlwyd to locate a clear path on the other side.

**6.** Todd has a snack by Bochlwyd with the Glyders ridge above and Gribin Ridge over to your right, this is a great place. If you are early you may find campers around this area.

**8.** Don't be tempted left too soon but continue on over a rocky knoll to cross the stream. Just after the stream turn left onto a faint grassy path and follow it around the foot of the outcrops.

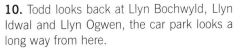

**7.** Continue on the clear path heading up between Tryfan and Bristly Ridge.

**10.** Todd looks back at Llyn Bochwyld, Llyn Idwal and Llyn Ogwen, the car park looks a long way from here.

**9.** As a scree slope comes into view ahead turn right and head up between the outcrops, you will need your hands here and there as well as a bit of help for your dog, scratch marks on the rocks will guide you.

**11.** As the boulders are left behind for a while a scree path develops which leads directly to a wall on the South Ridge.

**13.** There is no easy route from here, just a mix of scree and rock, Todd has a knack of picking the best route even if he does need a lift here and there.

**12.** Don't cross the stile, you will return here later. This is a nice spot to have a breather before climbing the final section to the summit.Follow the base of the slabs on the left of the stile to locate a rough path up between the rocks.

**14.** You will never take the same steps twice in this area but as a large rock formation appears above you pass it on the right and then bear left. The summit is not far away now.

You are near the Summit now please remember your route back down to the stile you just left. Tryfan is a beautiful but dangerous place, many people get lost up here and end up having to be rescued. Please don't try and descend by the North Ridge route especially if you have a dog with you, it is too easy to go astray and end up in some dangerous places, re- trace your steps to the stile and a pleasant return journey awaits you.

The day Todd did this climb was warm, we started walking at 5-30am and Todd was back, snoring in his bed, before it got too hot. On the same afternoon a Mountain Rescue Team had to rescue a German Shepherd from the North Ridge, trapped on difficult ground, too hot and exhausted. This is the wrong mountain for certain dogs and far too hot on that particular day. Please give Tryfan and the Rescue Teams the respect they deserve, have a safe journey back down.

**15.** Todd takes a breather in front of Adam and Eve.

**16.** A proud Todd poses on Eve with his new found friend Zack on Adam. Stunning views and huge drops behind the summit, a very early start on a weekday and you may have it all to yourself. Re-trace your steps (as near as possible) back down to the stile in picture 12. Dangerous ground on your left here, be careful.

**17.** Back at the wall, cross the stile and drop steeply towards Cwm Tryfan.

**18.** As the crags run out on your left look for a cairn by a big flat slab, turn left here and you are on the Heather Terrace, a good path that is a little awkward in places but worth the effort for the views all the way along it.
*\* Alternatively you could continue down the scree to reach a good path in Cwm Tryfan, turn left and you will eventually reach the stile in picture23.*

**19.** Todd on the Heather Terrace looking down at Little Tryfan and the A5 below. This path can be busy at weekends and you may

find climbers high above you taking routes that are out of bounds to walkers. You may also encounter Goats in this valley who can be confrontational if they have young and you have a dog with you, give them respect.

**20.** Lower down you will come to a scree slope heading down towards Little Tryfan, ignore this and continue on the small winding path the other side of the scree.

**21.** After a short sharp drop you come to the top of a gully, head down the gully to reach a grassy saddle.

**22.** Ignore two stiles on your right and continue by the fence.